3.38

D1122833

ANCIENT CHINA

A WALCK ARCHAEOLOGY

Editor: Magnus Magnusson

Ancient China

JOHN HAY

Illustrated with photographs and maps and with drawings
by ROSEMONDE NAIRAC and PIPPA BRAND

HENRY Z. WALCK, INC. New York

FRONTISPIECE
The sage Vimalakirti,
a Buddhist figure who
was adopted by the
Chinese as an image of
the ideal scholar. From
a wall-painting in the
Tun-Huang caves,
eighth century AD.

Library of Congress Cataloging in Publication Data
Hay, John, date-
  Ancient China.
  (A Walck archaeology)
  SUMMARY: Discusses the development
of archaeology as a discipline in China and
the remarkable facts it has revealed about
ancient Chinese civilizations and ways of life.
  1. China—Antiquities.   2. Archaeology.
[1. China—Civilization.   2. Archaeology]
I. Title.
DS715.H35 1974   913.31'03   73-15528
ISBN 0-8098-3530-4
ISBN 0-8098-3808-7 (pbk.)

ISBN: 0-8098-3530-4 (hardcover)
ISBN: 0-8098-3808-7 (paperback)
Library of Congress Catalog Card Number: 73-15528
Printed in Great Britain

CONTENTS

ACKNOWLEDGMENTS

Thanks are due to the following for permission to reproduce black and white photographs: Routledge & Kegan Paul Ltd for a photograph on page 27 from *Children of the Yellow Earth* by J. Gunnar Andersson; Ray Sutcliffe, in association with the BBC and the Times and Sunday Times Newspapers Ltd, pages 39, 52, 85, 110; Professor William Watson, pages 63 and 74; the Royal Society of London, page 25; Macmillan & Co Ltd for a photograph on page 108 from *Ruins of Desert Cathay* Vol. II by Sir Aurel Stein; Kodansha International, Tokyo, page 121. For permission to use coloured photographs thanks are due to Ray Sutcliffe, in association with the BBC and the Times and Sunday Times Newspapers Ltd, for the jacket and the illustrations facing pages 64, 81, 96 and 113.

The following photographs are reproduced from Chinese publications: black and white, pages 9, 11, 14, 19, 32, 37, 45, 49, 55, 59, 69, 71, 80, 84, 87, 93, 94, 95, 98, 99, 106, 111, 115 and frontispiece; colour, facing pages 65, 80, 97, 112.

The extract on page 99 is taken from David Hawkes' translation of *Ch'u Tz'u Songs of the South* published by the Oxford University Press; that on page 114 from Edward Schafer's translation in *The Golden Peaches of Samarkand* published by the University of California Press; that on page 76 is adapted from *The Book of Songs* by Arthur Waley, published by Allen & Unwin; those on page 71 and 75 from Samuel Griffiths' translation of *Sun-tzu, The Art of War* published by the Oxford University Press. The quotation on page 12 is taken from *Lu Hsun* published by the Peking Foreign Language Institute; that on page 22 from *Children of the Yellow Earth* by J. Gunnar Andersson published by Routledge & Kegan Paul Ltd; that on page 107 from *Ruins of Desert Cathay* Vol. II by Sir Aurel Stein published by Macmillan & Co Ltd; and that on page 113 from *The Long, Old Road to China* by Langdon Warner published by the Harvard University Press. The translation of the first oracle inscription on page 53 is taken from Li Chi's *The Origins of the Chinese Civilisation* published by the University of Washington Press, and the second on the same page is adapted from William Watson's *China* published by Thames & Hudson Ltd. The writing of the three characters on page 53 is based on Cheng Te-k'un, in *Shang China* published by Heffer of Cambridge.

The map on page 16 is by Edgar Holloway. The drawings on pages 18, 30, 31, 41, 43, 44, 48, 51, 53, 62, 67, 79, 88, 89, 91, 97, 100, 104, 109, 113, 114, 116, 117, 118, 122, 123, 124 and 125 are by Rosemonde Nairac, and those on pages 54, 60, 61, 62, 65, 66, 72, 75, 77, 78, 81 and 83 by Pippa Brand.

INTRODUCTION

There is a popular assumption that China is a mysterious, enclosed, inscrutable land. China and the West have been well acquainted with each other for many centuries, yet today their attitudes to each other are as much a mass of mutual contradictions as they have always been.

In the thirteenth century several Westerners visited the court of the Mongol Khans who were then ruling over China. One of these, William of Rubruck, was a scholarly observer; another, Marco Polo, was an extravagant spinner of romance. The former has been largely forgotten, whilst the latter's fame survives undiminished; a fact that is typical of Western attitudes towards China.

Jesuit missionaries who reached China in the late sixteenth century were the first to open up a direct and extensive exchange of information. Several of them were scholars of high standing, but their values were, like those of the Chinese, extremely egocentric. Some aspects of China, like her highly sophisticated system of centralised government operating through an educated élite, impressed them deeply; while many others, such as her art, were scornfully dismissed. In the eighteenth century the Chinese emperor banished the Jesuits and intellectual concern with China's culture then rapidly declined in Europe, although the trade in such commodities as porcelain gave rise to the aesthetic fashion of chinoiserie. As the appreciation of things Chinese became more superficial, so did disapproval become more dogmatic. The Protestant missionaries, who largely succeeded the Jesuits, were more rigid and also saw mainly China's grimmer face: the harsh poverty of a struggling peasantry, an intense suspicion of foreigners with ulterior motives.

The Chinese in turn composed a contradictory image. The

Jesuits had become the Astronomers Royal before they were cut down. Later foreign emissaries were welcomed, but not as equals, only as bearers of tribute to their emperor, who was literally 'the First Under Heaven'. Trade was accepted, but only under rigid restrictions. In 1839 hostilities broke out between the Chinese and British authorities in Canton. Britain was becoming arrogant and aggressive in her expectations of commercial profit, through the illicit trading of opium in this case, and British naval power forced a treaty of concession whereby the Chinese were compelled to accept the opium against their will.

The 'Opium War', as it is called, was highly typical of its time and by the turn of the century most Chinese shared a hatred of Western nations, a hatred that flared up in nationalistic uprisings like the abortive 'Boxer Rebellion' of 1899. But whilst some Chinese rejected all that the Western nations brought, others felt that China had to reassess her own deep-rooted tradition and come to grips with a new world. In the twentieth century this attitude has been immensely complicated by the development of Communism in China, which gathered momentum in the 1920s. Communist thinkers were often the most intense in their dislike of the West, yet they realised most keenly the urgent need for reform. Out of such a history has come the ambiguous relationship between China and the West of today. There is no more a mystery of China than there is a mystery of Europe, but the tangled communications will take a long time to straighten out.

The two civilisations can come together in two ways; in a vision of the future and in a study of their past. The Chinese are a nation uniquely self-conscious about their history. Their tradition of historical scholarship, which goes back several centuries before Christ, was studied and extended in an unbroken process. China has never relied on any supernatural source of eternal and ultimate authority, such as the Christian tradition. The philosopher Confucius explicitly confined himself to human affairs; ultimate criteria came only from accumulated human experience. It was this essential reverence for and use of the past that gave Chinese culture its extraordinary continuity, though the actual events of her history have brought as many upheavals as those in most other lands.

The Chinese concern for history often approached the concept of archaeology, through antiquarianism. One major example was their close study of inscriptions on stone tablets and bronze vessels, which has a tradition of over a thousand years and includes many works on the discovery and location of inscribed objects. But in China, even

8

One of present-day China's leading palaeontologists, Woo-ju-kang, works with trainee archaeologists in the cave of Peking Man.

more than in the West, the concept of history was bounded by a literate society. What, then, could her historians say of 'history' before the written word? Prehistory, or even a history of the illiterate masses, did not exist.

Archaeology, for these reasons, has become one of the most important meeting grounds between China and the West. Its discipline is modern. It was not till the nineteenth century in Europe that there was any real understanding of how it could reveal the actual structure of a vanished community. It did not reach China until the twentieth century. Several explorer-archaeologists from England, France, Germany and Russia made fascinating discoveries along China's Central Asian border in the first decades of the century, but the earliest authentically archaeological discovery in China was made by a Swedish mining engineer, Gunnar Andersson, who was making a geological survey for the Chinese government. In the years around 1920 he was intimately involved in the discovery of, firstly, Jurassic flora and fauna, secondly the Yangshao culture of the Neolithic (New Stone) Age and thirdly 'Peking Man' of the Palaeolithic (Old Stone) Age.

It is significant that all these discoveries lay far back beyond the scope of China's traditional history and were made, initially, as the side-product of a wholly modern science like geology. Because of this, some Chinese rejected them as irrelevant, whilst others realised that here was a dimension so new that it need not even conflict with the old. Wu Gin-ding, who made an extensive study of Andersson's neolithic finds, discovered the later neolithic culture of Lungshan in 1928. In the same year the Chinese government founded Academia Sinica, the nation's first institute of modern academic sciences. Tung Tso-pin and some other scholars from Academia Sinica immediately took the bold step of applying the archaeological test to one of the most ancient periods of traditional history, the Shang dynasty (*c.* 1500–1000 BC). They were superbly successful and revealed China's Bronze Age, near the town of Anyang. Investigations of the sites of Peking Man and the Shang dynasty continued through the 1930s. Pei Wen-chung, working at the former, became China's leading palaeontologist, and Li Chi, Hsia Nai and others working at Anyang became her leading archaeologists. The growing number of archaeologists led to some half dozen other significant finds during the 1930s, mostly of Chou dynasty remains (*c.* 1000–250 BC).

China was invaded by Japan in 1937, and in a remarkable demonstration of cultural tenacity the Chinese moved the bulk of their administrative and educational institutions to the mountain-locked western provinces. Even before 1937, field archaeology had been made very dangerous by unsettled conditions and several archaeologists had lost their lives. Little was done during the Japanese occupation except, strangely, by the Japanese themselves. When Japan capitulated, the struggles between the Nationalist and Communist Parties of China broke out into full-blown civil war. It ended with the flight of the Nationalists to the island province of Taiwan and the establishment by the Communists of the People's Republic of China in 1949.

After the Communist triumph in 1949, excavations were begun again with extraordinary dispatch under the auspices of a reconstituted Academy of Sciences. In 1950, not only was another major find made at the ancient Shang capital at Anyang, but the whole picture of the Bronze Age was modified by the discovery of an earlier Shang city at Chengchow. Since then, further finds have revealed a wide pattern of Shang culture.

Excavations at Pan-p'o, the most important neolithic site in China. The archaeologists are using measuring grids to make detailed plans of house foundations.

The total number of archaeological sites recorded and studied in China is now enormous. The handful of pre-war sites of the Yangshao Neolithic pioneered by Gunnar Andersson has swelled to over a thousand. The most important one, at Pan-p'o, was found in 1953 and is now an archaeological showpiece. Its full-scale publication in 1963 is the greatest single contribution to prehistoric archaeology in East Asia. In an altogether different field, excavations such as that of the tomb of the princess Yung-t'ai of the T'ang dynasty, who died in 701 AD, have revealed wall-paintings which before were known only from the accounts of contemporary writers.

The range of discoveries is vast. Many of them have been made in the course of China's gigantic reconstruction programmes, which have been conducted with a reliance on massive manpower inconceivable in the West. But a labourer is much more observant than a mechanical excavator, and in China great stress is laid on the need for co-operation between archaeologists, workers, and soldiers of the People's Liberation Army. It is plain that China's many trained archaeologists have been given ample doctrinal justification for their work: every archaeological publication is prefaced with the words of Chairman Mao, often to the effect that the past must not be forgotten, but must serve the present.

In 1973 the Chinese government sent a great exhibition of archaeological treasures to Paris and London. These were explicitly finds made during the Great Proletarian Cultural Revolution of the late 1960s. When the Red Guards began to rampage through China in 1966, the country almost completely barricaded itself against the outer world. The Red Guards developed into a self-generating tidal wave of youthful political fanaticism, unadulterated and undirected, such as has never been seen before. They shouted of smashing every relic of traditional culture associated with the old emperors and their concubines, and everything tainted by the West. Not surprisingly, the West feared that China was becoming a cultural desert. For seven years the only publications to come out of China were purely political. Then, in 1972, the scholarly journals began to reappear. Great was the surprise to find articles and reports of archaeological work written and carried out during the Cultural Revolution. Kuo Mo-jo, head of the Chinese Academy of Sciences, wrote an interpretation of a find of oracle-bones from the Shang dynasty. Excavations of Han dynasty tombs of the second century BC, such as those at Man-ch'eng (the jade suit tombs) and Ma-wang-tui, provided unsurpassed riches of Han artistry. Dr Hsia Nai, Director of the Institute of Archaeology at the Chinese Academy of Sciences, wrote: 'During the Great Proletarian Cultural Revolution, China's archaeological workers have taken part in the revolutionary struggle and at the same time did much work in the field . . . Workers, peasants or soldiers promptly report ancient relics they find and co-operate fully with the archaeological teams which follow up these leads . . .' Western archaeologists have been particularly pleased to find that the technique of radiocarbon dating is now being practised.

Archaeology in China is a proud science, but its place in her society remains unique in terms of archaeology and the world. Perhaps the most telling comment on this was written in 1925 by one of the greatest of modern Chinese writers, Lu Hsun.

'Foreign archaeologists are arriving one after another. For a long time, too, Chinese scholars have been shouting: "Preserve our ancient culture!" . . . But a people unable to reform will not be able to preserve its old culture either . . . The Great Wall has long ceased to serve any purpose . . . The people of this great old nation are taking refuge in fossilised traditions . . . Some foreigners are very eager that China should remain one great antique for them to enjoy for ever . . . Our chief aims at present are: first, to exist; secondly, to find food and clothing; and thirdly, to advance . . .'

1

The Historical
Background

It would be absurd to attempt to summarise the whole history of
China in a few pages. The purpose of this introductory chapter is
simply to give an historical framework to the end of the T'ang
dynasty (907 AD) for the chapters that follow.

The earliest neolithic (New Stone Age) culture in China developed
around 6000 BC in what has been called the 'nuclear area' of North
China—the fertile loess ('yellow earth') lands of the middle reaches of
the Yellow River valley and the Wei River valley. Farming developed
in sizeable settled communities, and pottery vessels came into use.
This earliest neolithic culture is known as Yangshao, from the site
where it was first identified, and is remarkable for its painted pottery.

Around 2500 BC, the Yangshao neolithic culture was followed by
the Lungshan neolithic culture in the middle and lower reaches of
the Yellow River, where more complex agricultural communities
developed. The potter's wheel was now used for the first time,
making elegant black vessels with thin walls. Society became more
stratified—the first indications of class division—and warfare between
settlements became more common.

The Bronze Age developed in China in northern Honan province
around 1600 BC with the Shang dynasty, which was China's first
historical era. Traditional historians spoke of a Hsia dynasty that
preceded the Shang, but there is no evidence yet that it was more
than legendary. Under the Shang, class differentiation became very
marked; bronze was used only by an elite aristocracy, who lived in
great walled cities and exercised absolute authority over the peasants,
whose culture remained neolithic.

About the year 1300 BC, the Shang moved their capital from Ao

(modern Chengchow) to Yin (modern Anyang). Here they built great ceremonial centres which were consecrated by large-scale human sacrifice, and excavated royal tombs show that dead rulers took hosts of sacrificial victims to the grave with them, including whole chariot teams. The earliest known Chinese writing comes from this period, in the form of questions carved on bones used as oracles and names on bronze vessels. The exact dates of the Shang are still in dispute; in this book the dates favoured by the Chinese authorities are used.

The Chou were an advanced, bronze-using tribe who lived in the Wei River valley. They repeatedly attacked the Shang state, and in 1027 BC (this is the revised date accepted by Chinese historians) they finally overthrew it and set up China's first feudal empire, the Chou dynasty (1027–256 BC). The Chou capital was established near modern Sian, but in 771 BC it was destroyed by invaders and was moved eastwards to Loyang, in Honan province. From this point onwards the various feudal territories began to erode the Chou emperors' authority. This period is known as the Spring and Autumn Era (772–481 BC), due to an historical account of it called the *Spring and Autumn Annals*, said to have been edited by Confucius (551–479 BC). Confucius, 'China's Greatest Teacher', was a teacher and scholar who travelled around the feudal states hoping to be employed as an adviser. Although much respected, he never achieved this ambition; yet he was the greatest of a series of great philosophers who lived during these centuries, known as China's finest age of philosophy, and his practical teachings on ethics and government were later adopted as an absolute standard of Chinese civilisation.

Confucius had praised the first Chou rulers as models of virtue, and lamented the decline of the emperors' authority; but after his lifetime North China deteriorated even more into a vicious struggle for power between the feudal territories, which had become independent states (Warring States Era, 402–221 BC). The Iron Age had now developed in China, which gave added impetus to warfare. There was also a flourishing development of commerce, based on such industries as iron and salt. Many walled market towns were built, and became very prosperous, to be fought over by the competing states. Walls were built along the frontiers, especially in the north, from where nomad tribes often attacked. The Chinese defended these walls with a new invention, the crossbow, and learned from the nomads a new technique of warfare, fighting on horseback. Previously horses had only been used for drawing chariots.

Gradually, one state emerged as the most powerful of the feuding

The Yellow River, heavy with sediment from the hills of terraced loess on either side, flows eastwards into the Central Plains. This is the heartland of ancient China, out of which spread the neolithic revolution.

15

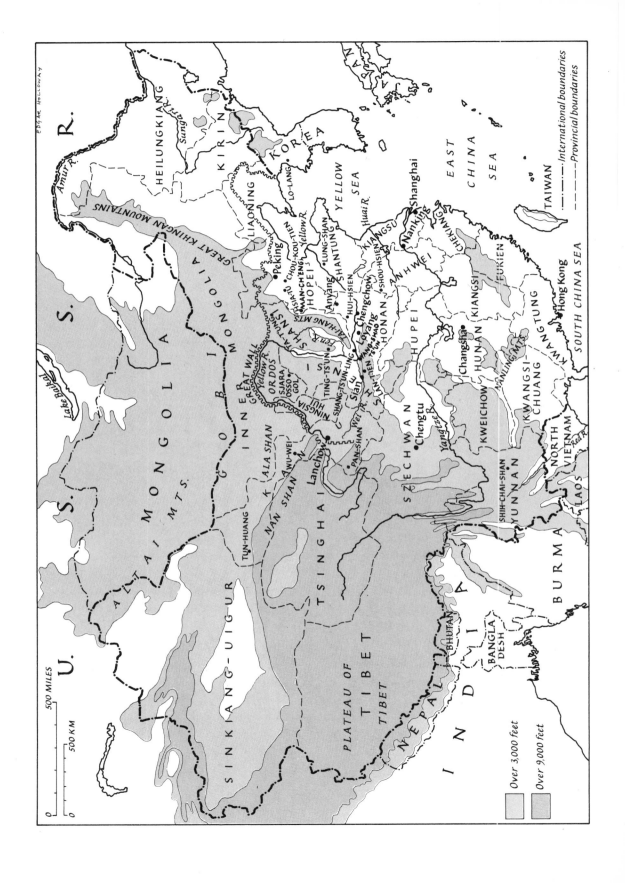

territories, the state of Ch'in, in the north-west. In 256 BC it finally destroyed the last of the Chou emperors, who was by now only a puppet, and by 221 BC it had subdued all the other states and established the Ch'in dynasty (221–206 BC), China's first unified empire. It was the first Ch'in emperor who joined up all the various frontier walls in the north to form the Great Wall of China.

The Ch'in dynasty was soon overthrown, and was succeeded by the long and glorious Han dynasty (206 BC–9 AD and 23–220 AD). The nomad tribes were for a time defeated, and Chinese forces marched far into Central Asia. Through this region ran the vital Silk Road, carrying China's most famous commodity on its way to the markets of the Roman Empire. The Han began to develop a civil bureaucracy, and scribes used brushes and ink to write a script which is very close to that of modern China. The cult of Confucianism began to form, and the Grand Historian of the Han court around 100 BC wrote a history of the world as he knew it; his name was Ssu-ma Ch'ien, and his work is the most famous historical work ever written in China.

In 9 AD the throne was briefly usurped by Wang Mang (Hsin Dynasty, 9–23 AD) but in 23 AD the Han were restored, and were known as the Later Han dynasty, to differentiate them from the Former Han dynasty. But they never quite recaptured their former glory. Bureaucracy flourished, and that great ally of bureaucracy, paper, was invented around 100 AD. About this time, too, Buddhism was introduced into China from India. It was not received with much enthusiasm at first, but it gained an ever-growing number of adherents as the Han empire began to disintegrate into chaos.

In 221, the Han empire was finally split up into the Three Kingdoms (221–280). From 265 to 316 there was a Western Chin dynasty, but it was the Eastern Chin dynasty (317–420) that left its mark, particularly in the fine arts. The Eastern Chin controlled only South China. The north at this period was divided into sixteen separate kingdoms, but the unified south saw a classic flowering of poetry, calligraphy and painting, and a development of theories of aesthetics.

The Eastern Chin were followed by an era known as the Southern Dynasties (four dynasties between 420 and 589) which saw a considerable intellectual development of Buddhism; while in the north there was the era of the Northern Dynasties (the Northern Wei and four minor dynasties, 386–581).

In the north, the nomadic tribes had come into their own again, and it was they who now ruled (Northern Wei, 386–535). But as time went by, they steadily became more Chinese. Partly for political reasons they patronised Buddhism, which flourished exceedingly. This was the great age of Chinese Buddhism and Buddhist sculpture. Under imperial patronage, massive temples were carved out of cliffs at Yun-kang in the latter half of the fifth century. In 494 the Wei capital moved to Loyang in Honan province, and another great cave-temple complex was begun in the cliffs at nearby Lung-men. A century or so earlier, the beginning of several hundred cave-temples with wall-paintings had been made at Tun-huang, an outpost on the route to Central Asia which was now carrying a large traffic of Buddhist monks. In North China a great number of inscribed stelae (monuments) were erected, promoting a special style of calligraphy which later became the major alternative to the classic style of the Eastern Chin. It was also in this era that gunpowder was invented and first used in firecrackers.

In 581, North China fell under the control of the Sui dynasty; in 580 the Sui reunited North and South China and re-established the Empire. The Sui dynasty was short-lived (589–618), but the dynasty to which it gave way brought one of China's most glorious eras, the T'ang dynasty (618–907).

The T'ang dynasty has been called China's Golden Age. After the centuries of division, China was unified again. The imperial court had immense prestige and attracted tribute from countries as near as Japan, as far as Persia. The capital was at Ch'ang-an (modern Sian, in Shensi province), and the Japanese built their own capital as a

Taoist Immortal riding on a crane. Wall-painting from Tomb of the Four Spirits, Chian, Chilin province, sixth century AD.

Silver box from the treasure of the Prince of Pin, Sian, *c* 700 AD.

replica of it. Large quantities of T'ang ceramics were exported by land and sea to the Middle East, and Middle Eastern metalwork brought back to China introduced new variety to Chinese design. Commerce flourished, education expanded, the examination for entry into the civil service (the only respectable career) was more broadly based. The stage was set for the decline of the ancient aristocratic families and their replacement by a new social order. There was great religious tolerance; Confucian state temples were established, and Hsuan-tsang, China's most celebrated Buddhist pilgrim, made an epic journey to India (629–645), bringing back new enlightenment and understanding.

It was an age of great artists and great statesmen, sometimes flourishing and sometimes suffering under rulers like the formidable Empress Wu in the latter half of the seventh century and her grandson, the 'Enlightened Emperor' in the first half of the eighth.

But by the middle of the eighth century, the T'ang glory had passed its peak. The Chinese were heavily defeated by the Arabs on their western borders. The Enlightened Emperor himself lost control of the reins of government, and in 755 he fled into exile when a favourite general, An Lu-shan, revolted and marched on the capital. An Lu-shan was eventually put down, but the restored T'ang dynasty never fully recovered. Religious tolerance declined. In 845, Buddhism was proscribed, resulting in a mass destruction of temples and sculpture. By the beginning of the tenth century, the Golden Age of the T'ang had come to an end.

CHRONOLOGICAL CHART

PERIODS AND DYNASTIES	DATE	KEY FACTS
NEOLITHIC YANGSHAO CULTURE	*c.* 6000 BC	First farming settlements in North China Grey and painted pottery
NEOLITHIC LUNGSHAN CULTURE	*c.* 2500 BC	More complex settlements Potter's wheel. Advanced black pottery
HSIA dynasty	?	Traditional only—no archaeological verification
SHANG dynasty	?1523–?1027 BC	Bronze Age. First historical dynasty
	?1300 BC	Shang capital moved to Anyang Royal tombs, chariots Earliest Chinese script
CHOU dynasty	?1027–256 BC	Start of feudalism
	771 BC	Capital moved to Loyang
Spring and Autumn Era	772–481 BC	Chou emperors lose authority
	551–479 BC	Confucius
Warring States Era	402–221 BC	Age of great philosophers Iron Age, much warfare between states Prosperous market towns Wars with nomads, frontier wall building
	256 BC	State of Ch'in destroys last Chou emperor
CH'IN dynasty	221–206 BC	First unified empire Great Wall of China
FORMER HAN dynasty	206 BC–9 AD	Civil bureaucracy Ssu-ma Ch'ien's *Records* Silk trade Military expeditions to Central Asia
HSIN dynasty	9–23	Wang Mang usurps throne
LATER HAN dynasty	23–220	Restoration of Han throne Buddhism introduced from India Introduction of paper
Three Kingdoms Era	221–280	Han empire split up
WESTERN CHIN dynasty	265–316	

EASTERN CHIN dynasty	317–420	Control of South China only
		Classic flowering of fine arts
Southern Dynasties Era	420–589	Liu Sung, 420–479 Southern Ch'i, 479–502 Liang, 502–557 Ch'en, 557–589
Northern Dynasties Era	386–581	Northern Wei, 386–535 Four minor dynasties North China ruled by nomads Buddhism flourishes: cave-temples and sculptures Gunpowder invented
SUI dynasty	589–618	Empire re-established
T'ANG dynasty	618–907	China's Golden Age, great international prestige Fine porcelain and pottery Extensive trade with Middle East
	629–645	Hsuan-tsang's pilgrimage to India
	755	An Lu-shan's rebellion: emperor in exile
	845	Buddhism proscribed, temples destroyed
Five Dynasties and Ten Kingdoms	907–960	
SUNG dynasty	960–1126	China re-unified
CHIN dynasty	1127–1234	Tartars occupy North China
SOUTHERN SUNG dynasty	1127–1279	Chinese rule driven down to the Yangtze River
YUAN dynasty	1279–1368	Mongol dynasty under the Great Khans Capital at Tatu (modern Peking) Visits of William of Rubruck and Marco Polo
MING dynasty	1368–1644	China's last native dynasty
CH'ING dynasty	1644–1911	The Manchus
Chinese Republic	1912–1949	
People's Republic of China	1949–	

2

Peking Man and
the Old Stone Age

The name Peking is associated with one of archaeology's most exciting discoveries: Peking Man, who lived nearly half a million years ago. The meaning of the city's name is 'Northern Capital' and it has been applied by the Chinese to the major city in the far north-east of their country whenever it has been their seat of government, as it is today.

Peking fostered an ever-growing foreign community in the early decades of this century. It was joined in 1914 by a young Swedish geologist called J. Gunnar Andersson, who had been invited by the government of the new Chinese Republic to assist in a major geological survey. Andersson, a man of thick-set physique and powerful personality, was destined to play an important role in China's discovery of her stone-age past. He later published, in 1934, an enthralling saga of the preceding twenty years, called *Children of the Yellow Earth*. He wrote of its contents: 'Nobody but I can relate how the discoveries were made . . . I feel it to be my duty to relate how all these investigations began on a small scale, how they grew and branched out, because I alone am in possession of the whole development of the story.' This was not a lordly gesture of claim over all the glory, for he gave due credit to many others, both Chinese and Western. The remark simply reflected the unique position that had been granted to him. It was he who found the first neolithic (New Stone Age) site in China, but he also played a leading role in discovering palaeolithic (Old Stone Age) man.

Andersson was prospecting for geological conditions which invited mineral exploitation. To this end he travelled extensively through China and was favoured with ready co-operation from the government. A principal interest of his own was to explore the geophysical history of China's land, and his contributions to this were considerable. But his interest in archaeology was growing all the time, and here the superb knowledge he gained of China's physical being was to stand him in good stead. With his own hands he crumbled her soil and scratched her rock. His eyes examined the succeeding millennia of growth revealed by the cut of cliff and canyon. In person he travelled the thousands of river miles which drained her floods and fertilised her fields. He pondered their meaning and visualised their ancient forms. Archaeology depends greatly on changes in the earth's face, on the mantling of things by soil for their preservation, on traces of this process for their discovery and interpretation. Man's evolution became far simpler to reconstruct when his changing environment was understood.

Andersson studied closely the region around Peking. The city lies in the north-west of a dry, flat plain that stretches towards the Yellow River in the south-east. A view from the tiled walk along the great city walls reveals a famous relief from this bland landscape. From the east to the south-west circles a blue line of hills. Those to the west have long been host to many temples and retreats. For centuries they have also produced stone for the city's buildings and coal for her fires. The coal mines were Andersson's first destination in 1914, and he found there perfect imprints of plants from the Jurassic Age, when giant dinosaurs trudged the earth. He also investigated the granite quarries in the limestone western hills near the small town of Chou-kou-tien, twenty-six miles south-west of Peking. These great ranges of hills were formed some hundred million years ago by shattering upheavals in the earth's crust, lifting through the vast and level expanse of fern-forest swamps in which the dinosaurs lived. Interminable washing waters had cut into folds and fissures, eroding deep caves. Over millions of years such caves trapped and preserved the debris of succeeding ages.

Andersson soon completed his first survey at Chou-kou-tien. But in 1918 he returned. At this time he was pursuing remains of the recently identified mammalian fauna of the Pliocene Age, (ten to two million years ago). An amateur archaeologist had been led to Dragon Bone Hill, a spot above Chou-kou-tien village and so called because it bristled with small bones. He told Andersson, who paid it a prompt visit, and found a great column of red clay left standing in a quarry. The quarriers had cut around the clay, leaving what had been a cave deposit as an isolated column. The clay was the typical deposit of the Pleistocene Age, which followed the Pliocene and marked the appearance of modern forms of life. This was too recent for Andersson's interests at that time. He was delighted at the bones, which were the first fossilised bones he had found, but was disappointed that they were the remains of mere birds and mice. A few months later he was overwhelmed by the discovery of Early Pliocene fossils in the banks of the Yellow River in Honan province, and he temporarily lost interest in Chou-kou-tien.

The new discoveries were so exciting that Andersson wrote to his colleagues in Sweden for assistance. This arrived in 1921 in the person of Otto Zdansky, a young Austrian student of palaeontology (the science of extinct forms of existence). Dragon Bone Hill was selected as a suitable site for him to gain practice in field work under local conditions, where the language barrier, lack of facilities and frequency of armed banditry were all hazards that had to be overcome. Zdansky set off just as Dr Walter Granger, one of America's foremost palaeontologists, arrived in Peking on his way to join an American expedition to Mongolia, which was destined to make the first find of a dinosaur's egg. He offered to show Andersson their newly developed technique of preserving fossilised bones by bandaging them as soon as they were uncovered.

Andersson consequently took Granger to Chou-kou-tien, where they joined Zdansky at his field post in the local temple, always an hospitable institution in China. On their first visit to the site, a local man approached them with the comment that there were some much better bones to be found nearby. Andersson knew by experience that such local hints were often the key to unexpected rewards. The party packed their kit immediately and followed their volunteer guide. They found themselves in another abandoned quarry, 150 yards west of Chou-kou-tien railway station. In a steep limestone cliff they could see an opening, packed solidly with rocks and debris washed in by rain. After a few minutes' probing they were excited to find the jawbone of a pig. Within two days they had extracted many other such pieces, the remains of pig, deer, rhinoceros and other mammals. The next day they were stranded in the temple by a splendid demonstration of the torrential rains which had shaped the jagged contours of the western hills, and over glasses of whisky they examined the bones, wondering what they meant. Andersson and Granger finally left Zdansky to pursue the new excavation, while they themselves escaped by stripping nearly naked and wading breast-deep through the torrents to the station.

The hill at Chou-kou-tien in 1930, with the recently discovered cave of Peking Man in the centre. Later excavations removed the entire side of the hill.

The limestone cave proved an awkward dig. It was almost inaccessibly high in a nearly perpendicular cliff, but with the help of bamboo scaffolding and ladders Zdansky dug there for several weeks and made extensive finds of fossil bones. These were taken back to Peking for analysis, and were proved to be from animals that lived in the Early Pleistocene, the time when man was thought to have emerged. Interest was stirred by the fact that they contained very few complete skulls and still fewer complete skeletons. Had the animals been dismembered by someone for food? Many fragments of quartzite were also found. They looked like the results of natural breakage, but their sharp edges could easily cut. Was it possible that they had been deliberately chipped to make tools? From his unrivalled knowledge of China's geographical history, Gunnar Andersson knew that the Peking plain had originally been seventy yards higher than at present, at a level that would have provided easy access to the cave.

These inklings provoked Zdansky's return to Chou-kou-tien in 1923. He recovered a further mass of material, similar to the first collection. He also dug out a tooth which he interpreted as a molar from an ape. He took most of this material back to the research institute in Sweden for a thorough examination. In 1926 Andersson organised a meeting of scientists to welcome the Crown Prince of Sweden on a visit to China. The Prince, a man of considerable qualifications, was addressed by leading scientists on their latest discoveries, and Andersson himself presented the latest results reported from the laboratory research in Sweden. He was in no doubt that the most exciting report was from Zdansky: further examination of his material had produced another tooth, and his analysis of both teeth had now convinced him that they had belonged not to an ape but to a man.

Andersson's colleagues reacted quickly. A preliminary report was published that same year by Dr Davidson Black, a Canadian professor of anatomy teaching in Peking. Dr Grabau, Andersson's eminent colleague at the Geological Survey, coined a catching name for the creature now dimly apprehended: Peking Man.

The gathering of scientists for the Crown Prince's visit had given Andersson an opportunity to suggest that a major search of the Chou-kou-tien site be organised. There was some critical opposition to overcome. The existence of Peking Man depended solely on the identification of his teeth as man-like, primarily through the formation of root and crown and their theoretical location in the jaw, and this was naturally difficult. Nevertheless, plans went ahead under the auspices of the Chinese government, to whom would belong any material discovered. The Rockefeller Foundation would bear almost the entire financial cost, and Dr Black was to conduct all the scientific analysis of any finds relating to the sought-for creature. From the institute in Sweden came Dr Birger Bohlin to carry out the actual excavation.

Dr Bohlin began his dig on April 16th, 1927. At this time North China was in near chaos. Peking lay in an area bloodily disputed by some of the most powerful warlords of China, military dictators who in some cases had controlled for decades areas the size of England. The national army was in turn engaged against the private armies. Dr Bohlin had exchanged the comfort of Stockholm for a cave with gunfire round the corner and total uncertainty of what the next day might bring. He and his Chinese associates worked on in the cave unperturbed, laying bare an area fifty yards long and sixteen yards broad. Marking the whole into a grid of six-foot squares, they dug seventeen yards deep and sifted through 3,000 cubic yards of deposit. Work was scheduled to end on October 19th, with the onset of winter. At 6.30 on the evening of that day Bohlin appeared at Black's door in Peking, still in his digging clothes, covered in dust, beaming with delight. He held another tooth, discovered three days earlier and brought to Peking under conditions of considerable danger.

Black was enthusiastically impressed, both with the tooth and with Bohlin. The new find, though worn by chewing, was beautifully preserved. He published the results of a brilliant analysis the next

OPPOSITE
The first excavations of Peking Man's 500,000-year-old home. Otto Zdansky is standing on the left with Dr Granger facing him.

26

year. The tooth belonged to the same species as those found by Zdansky and there was no doubt of their human character. On the basis of these three teeth Dr Black postulated *Sinanthropus* (Man of China), a hitherto unknown species in man's evolution, with the sub-species *pekinensis*.

Andersson was writing his *Children of the Yellow Earth* while these bold proposals were being digested. Twice before its publication in 1934 he had to add to his chapter on Peking Man. In 1928 and then again in 1929 Black's vision was fulfilled by yet greater finds. A nest of *Sinanthropus* fragments was uncovered in 1928, ten yards above the 1927 tooth. It included the front of a lower jaw, small fragments of a skull and several more teeth. Black's comparisons showed a creature half-way in type between man-like ape and modern man.

Additional Chinese staff had now joined the excavation. One of these, Pei Wen-chung, headed the team which arrived in September 1929, as soon as the seasonal heavy rains had let up, and it was he who was to make the discovery that put Peking Man beyond dispute. He dug down to a depth of 73 feet, where he reached a branch in the cave. He was faced with a choice between two open holes. The one being inaccessible except on the end of a rope, he began to work through the deposit on the floor of the other. At four o'clock the following afternoon he came upon a cranium, almost complete. It was partly held by the porous rock which had formed around it. Pei chiselled out a block containing the skull and carried it to his quarters. There, in the manner which Dr Granger had showed to Zdansky, he wrapped it in the soft cotton-paper favoured by centuries of Chinese artists. Round this he further wrapped coarse cloth soaked in flour paste. The weather was so cold that even after three days in his heated room the paste had not set. Finally he surrounded the parcel with the charcoal table-cookers which perform so nobly during the grim winters in North China. When the paste was dry and the parcel safely hardened, Pei bore his uniquely precious burden through the same dangers that had attended Bohlin and his tooth, and delivered it at Black's laboratory.

The Chou-kou-tien site had a very particular importance. Other traces of primitive man had been discovered elsewhere, but in circumstances which told nothing of the kind of life he had led. Such, for example, were Neanderthal Man, found in a German lime-stone quarry in 1857; Java Man, dug from the Solo River bank in Java in 1890; Rhodesia Man, uncovered in a lead and zinc mine at Broken Hill in 1921. Chou-kou-tien was unique, for it was a dwelling site, very limited in extent and occupied over hundreds of millennia. Pei's continuing excavations produced, among other discoveries, traces of charcoal and charred bones. These are still the earliest evidence known of man's deliberate use of fire for cooking and eating. In the same year, 1931, he found the site's first associated examples of stone tools indubitably shaped by human hands.

So the Chou-kou-tien site presented, through the medium of archaeology, much more than earlier finds had offered. Here were skeletal remains for anthropologists to reconstruct its inhabitants; tools by which to assess their artifice and affiliations; animal remains for the zoologist to identify their contemporary fauna and prey; undisturbed strata for the geologist to see their landscape and for the botanist to find their covering plants and vegetable food. The site complex even provided a primitive guide to their community. The excavations lasted for over ten years, removing about 20,000 cubic yards of hillside, of which at least 8,000 were taken away and sifted. Fifteen distinct areas of occupation were identified. Locality 13 is the earliest and Locality 15 the latest. Locality 1 contained all the skeletal remains and the largest number of stone tools. Five nearly complete crania were found, along with 152 teeth and sundry other pieces of skeleton, representing at least forty men, women, and children.

Nearly all archaeological work in China came to a sudden end in July 1937, when a shooting incident engineered by the Japanese led to an immediate and massive invasion. Despite this, the scientists at Chou-kou-tien managed to continue their work until 1939. By 1941 the Chinese government was besieged in the mountain fastness of western China, and an agreement was made with the American authorities to transfer the *Sinanthropus* collection to the safety of the United States. Just at this moment the Japanese attacked Pearl Harbor. The crated fossils had reached a US marine base in a small harbour north-east of Peking. The base was in confusion. The crates vanished from mind and sight. They have never been seen since, a fact which more than rankles with the Chinese who feel that they should never have been allowed to leave the country.

The shock of this loss was mitigated by the plaster casts, photographs and careful studies already made and remaining at the Cenozoic Research Laboratory in Peking. Franz Weidenreich, a leading member of the staff, took his own material back to the United States and devoted his remaining career to its elucidation. When stability in China was eventually established by a Communist government in 1949, excavations at the site were resumed. A partial cranium,

Peking Man, from a reconstruction by Franz Weidenreich.

shin-bone fragments, a lower jaw and some teeth have since been found.

The discovery of Peking Man made a tremendous impact at the time, because he had been the first man found in a fully domestic environment. Since then, there have been further, equally dramatic, discoveries that have greatly illuminated (and sometimes complicated) our knowledge of man's evolution. Although still of major importance, *Sinanthropus* no longer plays a role of such dramatic splendour in our view of evolution. But he is understood much better.

He is now assigned to the Middle Pleistocene, 450,000 to 500,000 years ago, and is properly called *homo erectus pekinensis*. This means he is the sub-species *pekinensis* (of Peking), defined by place of discovery; of the species *erectus* (upright in stance), because of his similarity to Java Man who had been previously discovered and so named; and within the genus *homo* (man). *Homo* is the latest stage of an evolutionary family called the *hominidae*. It is thought that around thirty million years ago the zoological anthropoid suborder of higher primates divided into the two main branches of *pongidae* and *hominidae*, leading respectively to apes and monkeys and to man. Java Man, when first discovered, was called the 'missing link' between ape and man. The term is nowadays considered worse than useless, but in any case he was twenty-eight million years too late for such a claim. After twenty-eight million years of an often unsuccessful evolutionary process, a creature we call *Australopithecus* came down from the trees to live on the ground. His best known home, the Olduvai Gorge in Tanzania, has largely eclipsed the drama of Chou-kou-tien. He walked upright, but was only about four and a half feet high. Although his brain was only one third the size of ours, he understood tools and began to make them. About one million years ago he was superceded by *homo erectus*, whose brain was at first twice as big and who stood about a foot higher. Anthropologists find him close enough to ourselves to call him species *homo*.

Peking Man lived half a million years after his species first appeared. During the hundreds of millennia of his existence he seems to have changed not at all in appearance. His body and limbs, covered in hair, were very like ours in proportion. But his arms had developed faster than his legs. Some of the advantages of standing upright, such as looking over tall grass and intimidating quadrupeds, were enjoyed even by apes. But man's perfect balance and fast running required a very long and complex development. The head and face of Peking Man gave him a savage appearance. Large teeth were thrust well

Chou-kuo-tien

Ting-ts'un

Sjara Osso Gol

Three stages of
development in
palaeolithic tools.

forward on great jaws. He had no chin, but a broad, flat nose and a heavy, beetling ridge of bone above his eyes. A low forehead curved flatly back to a bulging occiput. His brain, bigger than that of Java Man, was on average slightly more than two thirds the size of ours. Crucial features of brain formation, more important than size, indicate he had the gift of speech.

Adherence to a dwelling site, communication through speech and affinity of fire all indicate at least a primitive form of society. The power of fire, which both draws a group together and separates it from others, may well have entailed an awakening of family relationships. It also affected diet, extracting recalcitrant calories from raw food and greatly increasing chances for survival. Peking Man, unlike the vegetarian ape, ate both plant and flesh. He was a notable hunter on the grasslands south-east of his cave where his major prey was a heavy-jowled deer with enormous sail-like antlers. To trap such a swift beast required an organised group of hunters, an important stage in human evolution. Hunting was also a male pursuit, and such a distinction must have been a major factor in the sexual differenti-ation of activities. Besides the deer and smaller animals, Peking Man ate his own fellows. The cave deposits revealed that he split their bones for nutritious marrow and carefully cracked their skulls for the succulent brain. In his turn he was the prey of sabre-toothed tigers from the thickly forested hills to the north-west.

The tools he used for crushing, digging and cutting were mostly primitive flaked-pebble choppers of quartz. Over a hundred thousand pieces associated with this lithic industry were found in Locality 1, scattered around ten successive layers of hearth. Some 'core tools' were made with large pebbles, by striking away chips from alternate directions. The majority were 'flake tools', struck off a larger stone with a single blow. The results were left in this coarse and irregular form. Stumbled across in isolation many would scarcely be recognised as tools. The later deposits, however, show some improvement in manufacturing technique. Shapes became more regular and cutting edges were sometimes roughly trimmed. They were often made from a smooth-textured flint, which is much more amenable than quartz.

The Chou-kou-tien occupation fell between two Ice Age glacials. Pollen analysis, a new and very effective technique, has shown that whilst the mean average temperature at that time was lower than at present, it rose considerably higher in the middle of the period. The surrounding forests changed accordingly. In the middle phase they were greatly varied by temperate species such as oak, ash and elm.

31

The variations of both temperature and vegetation must have affected Peking Man's life. The latterly increasing cold is the only known element possibly connected with his otherwise unexplained departure.

Franz Weidenreich analysed a number of Peking Man's features, such as the shovel-like shape of his incisors, which strongly suggest features of the modern Mongolian race. The possibility of this very interesting relationship, relevant to the question of whether man evolved independently in different parts of the world, has been reinforced by a skull found near Lan-tien in Shensi province in 1964. This very important skull is smaller and perhaps 200,000 years older than those found at Chou-kou-tien, being even more closely related to Java Man. But it is without a third molar and this is a congenital defect becoming more frequent in the Mongolian race today.

Lan-tien Man may be related to a culture along the middle and upper course of the Yellow River contemporary with the very earliest locality at Chou-kou-tien. What came before is largely unknown. The search often seems like a dentist's nightmare, with a tooth to be extracted from a mountain range. Teeth tend to be more widely scattered than their owner. They are well protected by enamel. Their forms are an extraordinarily effective witness to living habits. One anthropologist spent many years collecting fifty teeth from Hong Kong apothecaries, from which Weidenreich diagnosed a hominid

Left Restored skull and jaws of Lan-tien Man. The earliest anthropoid skull found in China. *Right* Skull cap and jawbone of Peking Man found at Chou-kou-tien after 1950. Partially restored.

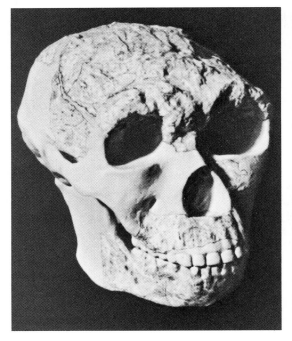

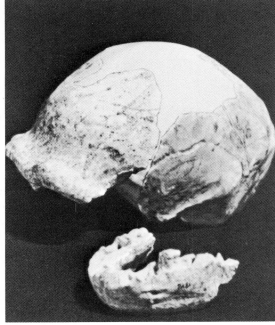

giant of the Pleistocene Age. Pei Wen-chung, still a leading authority in this pursuit, tracked the giant down to a cave high above a river in Kwangsi province. The cave yielded three jawbones of the creature and proved him to be a carnivorous ape with several man-like features. He lived some 500,000 years earlier than Peking Man and was doubtless an evolutionary blind alley.

The Late Pleistocene was the period of the Riss and Würm glacials in the European late Ice Age. Glacial movements have been traced across the Himalayas into West China, although they do not seem to have covered North China. But after Peking Man's habitation at Chou-kou-tien, an interval of genial climate gave way to cold and rain associated with another glacial to the west. This was followed in the late Pleistocene by an extraordinary development. Vast areas of rock had been eroded by ice and rain. The products were swept up by dry winds blowing over North China. Fine, yellow dust drifted and settled for thousands of years. When it ended, the landscape had been stifled under an accumulation up to three hundred feet thick. The land and the life upon it were irreversibly transformed. The deposit, covering the modern provinces of Kansu, Shensi and Shansi, is called loess. Not surprisingly, no traces of man have been found within the place and period of its accumulation, but there is steadily increasing evidence of life in the surrounding regions.

The most substantial finds have been in the Ordos, a Mongolian name for the grasslands through which the Yellow River reaches its northern extreme and turns east again. In the 1920s the region was explored by Jesuit scientists. Jesuits had introduced Western science to China in the seventeenth century and become the emperor's astronomers in the eighteenth. They were long the most remarkable, and controversial, group of Westerners in China. Father Emile Licent and Teilhard de Chardin, who explored the Ordos, rank with Andersson and Black as Western discoverers of prehistoric China. They revealed an Ordos Man who had evolved well beyond Peking Man. His tools, particularly from the Sjara Osso Gol site, are remarkable for their microblades—very small flakes neatly struck from a carefully prepared core. A small minority, such as the triangular scrapers, have had their edges strengthened by secondary chipping. These tools, associated with the lake and river-side communities in the north-west, are distinct from the chopper-flakes associated with forest-dwelling Peking Man and his successor Tingts'un Man, who was found some three hundred miles to the southwest. The subsequent development of lithic industries suggests that the microblade tradition spread more effectively.

This spread may have been a function of climatic change. When the last glacial had receded, North China was rejuvenated by warm sun and rains. Forests of large-leafed trees grew over the loess and the great Manchurian plains. The river and lake landscape of the prehistoric Ordos became more widespread. The woolly rhinoceros and mammoth, supreme in harsh glacial conditions, vanished from North China. Warmth-loving vegetation and animals migrated up from the south.

Man's evolution had become much faster as the Ice Age neared its end. He is first welcomed into the species of modern man, *homo sapiens*, about 300,000 years ago. His brain became as large as ours, sometimes much larger, but still encased in an ape-like skull. This character, called *neanderthaloid*, is seen in late pleistocene China with Ordos Man. About 50,000 years ago the man-like body was finally crowned with a man-like head. The cranium became tall and rounded, pushing forward over the ancient brow-ridge. A chin developed to balance the chewing action. *Homo sapiens* may well have originated in Northern Africa and Asia Minor. Whether he migrated into China, mixing with or displacing existing occupants, or whether he evolved independently in China, is a fascinating problem which the gathering pace of palaeontology in China may well solve.

At Chou-kou-tien, a cave higher up in the limestone hill has yielded remains of an 'upper caveman', physically extremely close to the modern Mongolian. Estimated at around 25,000 years old, he lived on the border between the Palaeolithic (Old Stone) and Mesolithic (Middle Stone) ages. Pei Wen-chung discovered the cave in 1930. It contained the remains of old men, women and children violently slain, their shattered skeletons sprinkled with red haematite dust. This is the earliest evidence of a burial rite in China. The ore for this powder must have come from beyond the mountains, at least a hundred miles to the north, which suggests that by now there was active commerce between widely separated communities. Another exclusively human concern, dressing up, is witnessed here in China for the first time by painted beads, tooth pendants and shell ornaments. Here at last we recognise our fellow man.

3

Farmers and Painted Pots: Neolithic China

'The Chinese have never passed through an epoch which for other culture regions has been designated as a Stone Age.' These were the words, written in 1912, of a leading historian of Chinese art.

That historian and many of his contemporaries found the sophistication of the most ancient Chinese tradition then known impossible to relate to 'primitive' man. Had they known of Peking Man, they would have argued that he had been a savage in a local tribe, vanished without issue into mists of prehistory. But scholars such as De Chardin and Andersson were searching these mists. Early in the 1920s interest in a Chinese neolithic period was aroused. De Chardin's discovery of the Ordos culture and other related finds were opening some distant vistas. But the biggest challenge was to discover a true Neolithic Age for the peoples of Central China.

The Neolithic was an age of immense importance. Its transformation of the wandering hunter into a sedentary farmer was a revolution as vast and profound as that of the Industrial Age. It was known that the process had occurred in eastern Europe and westwards during the sixth and fifth millennia BC. No major civilisation could have arisen without a permanent foundation to its house, both actual and metaphorical. The household itself could not have been supported without the ability to keep on producing food in the same area. Chinese tradition acknowledged this in the mythological emperor Shen Nung, who 'created agriculture and pottery'.

Andersson often depended on a team of five Chinese 'collectors'. These men scoured the country for the objects of his current interest. In the fall of 1920 he sent one of these men to a district in Honan province, looking for further signs of the pleistocene mammal fossils first noticed two years before. The collector was also to watch out for neolithic remains. After a couple of months he returned to Peking and amazed Andersson with a collection of several hundred stone tools. They were advanced in type and well preserved. The collector had found them near a small village called Yang-shao-ts'un. Five months later, Andersson took a train to the nearest town and set off along the six-mile walk to the village. Just south of his destination the road cut across a deep ravine, where a clear vertical section through the ground was revealed. Andersson's attention was suddenly caught by a layer of ashy soil, lying above the red tertiary clay and containing fragments of pottery. Suspecting that this was the culture stratum from which his collector had obtained the stone tools, Andersson began poking around. In a few minutes he found something quite unexpected. It was a piece of fine, red pottery, with its surface highly polished and painted with a black pattern. Andersson, to use his own words, was 'rather depressed'. Whatever the origins of the ashy soil, it surely could have no connection with neolithic tools.

He decided to spend the visit making a geological survey, convinced that his neolithic hopes had been dashed. Yang-shao-ts'un lies in a valley which runs parallel with and south of the Yellow River. It is in the south-eastern extremity of the vast loess field which spreads over north-west China. The Tsinling mountain range, which can be seen from Yang-shao-ts'un stretching from east to west, was a barrier to the southwards spread of the loess. The almost treeless, relentlessly yellow-brown loessic landscape has been one of the most characteristic faces of Chinese history. Since it was laid, the blanket of dust has shifted and cracked, opening up sheer ravines and towering, vertical cliffs. Rain pouring through the cracks washes yellow mud into the rivers. Northern China's greatest river curves through the entire length of the loess field, burdened with this mud. Hence it is called the Yellow River. In the east the mud has been redeposited, forming vast plains of so-called secondary loess. The ceaseless silting has raised the river to innumerable cataclysmic floods. Hence it is also called China's Sorrow. But man has carved and is still carving the slopes of loess into seemingly endless successions of terraced fields. For loess is both cruel and benign. When warm rains come, capillary action in the soil draws nutrient minerals rapidly to the surface and crops flourish strongly. But drought can bring death to the land with equal speed, while torrential rains can wash away great chunks of the landscape overnight.

Funerary urn from a
late Yangshao site in
Kansu province. These
urns were placed
around the corpse,
which was curled on
its side.

Andersson spent two days examining this fascinating geological history, while village lads, eager to make a few cents, continually brought him stone tools. On the third day he felt driven to a thorough search of the ravine walls. Eventually he found a stone adze clearly located in the same ashy stratum as some fragments of painted pottery. He also realised that this stratum was very extensive and rich with a wide variety of objects. He returned to Peking with the mystery of Yang-shao-ts'un's painted pottery at the back of his mind. In the library of the Geological Survey he happened on a publication of the Pumpelly expedition to Russian Turkestan in 1903 and 1904. Its illustrations of finds from a late neolithic site included pottery painted with designs which reminded him instantly of the fragments from Yang-shao-ts'un. Only now did the possibilities of his discovery dawn on him. He suggested an excavation to his superiors and was lucky that the Chinese government had decided that the Geological Survey was the best institution to tackle all surveys, whether geological or archaeological. Within six months he was back at Yang-shao-ts'un with an efficient Chinese staff, and he was also joined for a while by his expert associates, Davidson Black and Otto Zdansky. Their great precision in excavation technique was much valued by Andersson and was surely a factor in the high standard of field work which came to characterise Chinese archaeology.

The excavations lasted five weeks. The speed with which Andersson swept through even his most important discoveries has shocked many modern archaeologists, for scientific excavation is now a painstaking and long drawn-out operation. Even so, what Andersson achieved was to reveal a true neolithic culture in China for the first time, and the extent and richness of the remains astonished Andersson's team. They indicated a community which would have been extraordinary for such an inhospitable spot in the Stone Age, but the geological surveys being conducted at the same time provided a surprising answer. The riven loess and inaccessibility of streams at the bottom of the ravines were more recent phenomena. When neolithic farmers were cultivating the loess, the water level had been so much higher that rivers had flowed near the surface of the plateau. The vegetation had been totally different, too, with thick forest covering much of the ground.

Yang-shao-ts'un was one of those discoveries which make it seem that archaeology and prehistory are the same thing. For the excavations raised the curtain on another scene in China's past, a scene which previously had not even appeared in the script. As the number of properly identified sites subsequently increased, the culture associated with the painted pots became known as the Yangshao culture, named after the village of Yang-shao-ts'un. Andersson's fame rests most securely on its identification, but not even he suspected how extensive its revelations were to prove.

More than a thousand Yangshao sites are now known, dating, it is believed, from 6000 to 4000 BC. Further discoveries moved the known centre of this culture further west and showed that the original Yang-shao-ts'un site was a late phase. Excavations conducted mostly after 1950 have located over four hundred sites along the Wei River valley. This extends for about two hundred miles westwards from where the Yellow River turns sharply eastwards. Neolithic habitation in this area was almost as dense as it is today. One site, at Hua-yin, has a known extent of over a million square yards. The largest excavation, at Pan-p'o-chai, has made the greatest single contribution to our knowledge of neolithic Asia.

Pan-p'o-chai is a small farming village, four miles south-east of Sian, the famous old capital city of Shensi province. It lies against a loess terrace above a small tributary running north into the Wei River.

This section of the Wei valley, bounded on the south by the Tsinling Mountains thirty miles distant, has the densest of all Yangshao concentrations. Many sites occur in pairs, facing each other across a river. In 1953 a team responsible for maintaining cultural remains in north-west China was led to traces of a neolithic settlement on the long, low terrace above Pan-p'o-chai, where foundations for a factory were being dug. In the following year an investigation was mounted by the Chinese Academy of Sciences. It was immediately apparent that unusually substantial remains lay hidden there, and by the autumn of that year an excavation team of over a hundred men was at work under the direction of Dr Hsia Nai from the Academy. They continued work through five sessions, concluding in the summer of 1957. By then they had thoroughly worked over an area of 14,000 square yards. They had also probed the outlying area and found that the excavated area was less than a quarter of the total site. The site has been preserved under cover as a major archaeological showpiece open to the public.

The Pan-p'o site as it is preserved for exhibition, showing house foundations with rows of holes for supporting posts.

The site as known at present approximates a rectangle, its longer sides on a north-south axis. It is about 60,000 square yards in extent, although the north-west corner has been destroyed by erosion and

farming. The area is very flat, relieved by an occasional stumpy tree, the ancient remains filled by drifting loess and smoothed by continuous cultivation. Typical of the Sian district, the ground is pierced by many graves of a later date, mainly from the fifth century BC through to the ninth century AD. Several of these were found in a particularly deep section of post-neolithic deposit. This turned out to be the filling of a huge trench some twenty feet deep and twenty-three feet broad. Exploratory probing followed it along a great curve that enclosed the site's north-western half.

The enclosure covered 35,000 square yards and was bounded on the west by the descending terrace slope. The great trench was probably defensive, for the enclosed area contained foundations of a village. The peculiar qualities of the loessic ground had been put to fascinating use by the neolithic villagers, and they were, in turn, of great advantage to the archaeologists. Loess clings together with a very homogeneous texture, remaining firm even on a vertical surface. It is almost sculpturally amenable to shaping. Although its homogeneity obscures distinctions between successive layers, it preserves well the shape of buried objects. The excavators uncovered a complex pattern of pits and holes. They sorted this out into two main features: house foundations and storage pits. The Yangshao farmers had carved the floors of their houses out of the ground, sometimes digging as deep as three feet. These pits and their many accompanying post-holes were preserved by the firm loess, often to extraordinarily vivid effect.

Forty-six house foundations were excavated and of these Number 41 is a very good example. This house had plainly been burnt down and the floor pit was still strewn with the charred roof-timbers. The floor was fifteen feet long and ten feet wide, dug about eighteen inches below ground level. A long entrance passage sloped in from the south side, ending with a low platform just inside the pit. The platform was surrounded with a low rim, obviously to keep out water. Post-holes surviving in other examples of this rim show that a partition formed an enclosed hallway. Near the centre of this snug home was a shallow, round hearth-pit. On either side were recesses for two upright roof-supports, their bases surrounded with clay as a protection against the fire. The roof timbers, as revealed by their charred remains, once sloped up directly from the ground around the pit and were thatched with reeds and clay. Some other houses have the practical addition of a low retaining wall around the rim of the pit. Many have neat storage niches carved out of the pit walls. Jars still stood in some of these. A jar on the floor of house Number 41 contained snail shells.

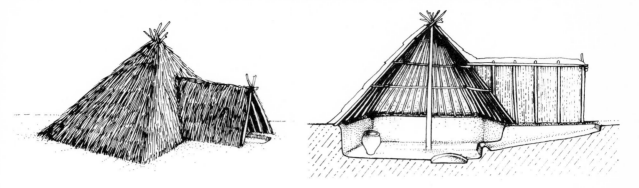

Reconstruction of pit house Number 41 from the early level of Pan-p'o, sixth millennium BC.

Many house-pits overlapped each other, successive generations having built on the remains of their predecessors. Some houses were round and others were quadrilateral. Both forms were divisible into an earlier and a later type, a relative chronology clearly shown by the succession of their foundations. Radiocarbon tests indicate that the earlier houses were built around 5000 BC. Later houses were often larger and not always sunk in a pit, with deeper, gourd-shaped hearth-pits and one half of the floor higher than the other. The houses all face south and, within contemporary groups, are regularly spaced at intervals of ten to fifteen feet. Amongst the later foundations is one of exceptional size. Its proportions approximate those of Number 41, but it is ten times as large. Foundations contemporary with it all seem to face it in a regular row on the north side. This strongly suggests the communal centre of a well-organised village. The large foundation is at the extreme south-west corner of the excavated area, so we cannot tell whether it was originally central to the whole site. But judging from the overall pattern of the site, the excavators felt that during its early period of occupation there must have been about six hundred people living in some two hundred houses.

Such a large and well-settled population not only needed to cultivate and gather large quantities of food. They needed to store it. The answer was another very characteristic feature of the site, over three hundred deep storage pits scattered among the houses. Some were as deep as six feet and almost all had a distinctive inverted-cone shape. They were made larger as occupation went on, with a base as wide as eight feet and a mouth of less than half that. Their sides were plastered smooth with clay. Like the pit-houses, these were examples of man and loess shaping each other.

Among the houses and often very close to their walls were found many infant burials. The corpses had all been sealed in two large jars joined mouth to mouth. Adults had been buried in a special cemetery, which was found in the north-west corner of the site during the second season of excavation. Burial rites are one of the best guides to ethnic affiliation and those at Pan-p'o, as the site is called, are the same as all others from the central area and main period of Yangshao development. Corpses were stretched out on their backs, heads to the north-west. An exceptional child-burial in the cemetery retained traces of the earliest coffin known in China. Of 174 cemetery burials, 71 contained funerary objects, mainly pots and ornaments such as beads and earrings. The pots, placed between the legs, usually occur in a particular combination and there was a trend towards a type of pot made especially for the rite. Archaeology has neither tools to discover, nor vocabulary to describe, the belief in whose image the rites operated. But how vastly has man's sense of both knowledge and ignorance flourished! His palaeolithic forbears had buried their dead underfoot in dwelling caves, an inkling of mystery expressed by scattering blood-red dust. Pan-p'o's clear and symbolic separation of the dead from the living is shared by all the Yangshao sites.

Pan-p'o revealed another specialised area, characteristic of the Yangshao culture. Clustered east of the houses and pits no fewer than six pottery kilns were found. Pottery is one of the most interesting neolithic features. A hunter's prey can simply be stuck in a fire and roasted. Porridge needs a pot. For this, a lump of clay can be squeezed into a rough container, or it can be turned elegantly on a potter's wheel. The result can be left to harden in the sun, or baked in an oven to make a vessel of extraordinarily durable material. The exceptional stability of ceramic ware makes it an invaluable form of evidence, although this has often made archaeologists seem wholly pot-bound.

The kilns at Pan-p'o were unexpectedly eloquent of Yangshao technology. They showed an efficient development of the basic requirement for high-temperature firing: a clear separation between the three stages of furnace, heat channel and firing chamber. They could have reached a temperature of over 1000°C. The pots themselves were still made by moulding strips of clay with hands and paddle. The finer specimens perhaps had their mouths shaped by slow turning. Pots made for general use and for burials were roughly but attractively finished with patterns of cord, net, woven fabric or even fingernail impressions. One common shape is a long oval with a pointed bottom; this was for gathering water and was kept hanging on the wall. Pots for fancier and ritual use, although with the same orange-red fabric, are finer in texture and have their surface burnished.

It is these which sometimes were painted with striking black designs.

The expressly 'neolithic' character of Pan-p'o is of course seen in the stone tools. The finest are masterpieces of stone-craft, perfectly shaped and beautifully polished. The commonest are adze-blades and reaping knives. Bone was also much used for a variety of small tools, such as needles, arrowheads and fish-hooks. Ornaments were often made from shell and precious stone.

The extensive storage pits and many sickle-knives show how busy were the farmers of Pan-p'o. Large deposits of grain in the pits have been identified as fox-tail millet, still the main crop of northern China. In the Yangtze region and further south rice is the main crop. This basic division evidently goes back to neolithic times. There is evidence of interruptions in the neolithic occupation of Pan-p'o, seen even more clearly at some other Yangshao sites. Pollen analysis of Pan-p'o deposits show that pollen of forest trees increased by about thirty per cent during two phases. This suggests that ignorance of soil conservation may have lead periodically to bad crops. Farmers would then have moved to another district, leaving the forest slowly to recover their old fields and the ground to be enriched by natural organic decay. After a cycle of many decades, the community would find itself back on old territory, reclearing the forests with their extremely effective stone adzes.

Many bones and a stock-pen foundation at Pan-p'o show that livestock also was reared, principally pigs and dogs. These animals, especially the pig, are still the most popular meat in China. A great deal of fishing activity in the Wei River valley settlements is shown by extensive fishing gear, such as net-sinkers and hooks. The importance of fishing hints at a connection in the distant past with mesolithic (Middle Stone Age) hunters and fishers of the Ordos region; but the origins of the Yangshao agricultural development is still one of the unsolved questions facing Chinese archaeologists. It is now thought that a number of sites in Shensi, characterised by a very coarse, cord-marked pottery, may represent a pre-Yangshao horizon.

Fishing is a semi-settled occupation which could well have led into farming. Its importance at Pan-p'o produced one of the very few pieces of archaeological evidence in which there is an unmistakeable, if elusive, link between the material culture and spiritual world of the Yangshao peoples. The majority of painted pots and their fragments found there have fish-form motifs. Pots from the latest levels have an apparently geometrical decoration which had, in fact, evolved very slowly from a perfectly intelligible fish seen on the earlier examples.

Polished stone adze from Pan-p'o with reconstructed handle.

The most fascinating motif is surely ritualistic, showing a human face behind a mask of multiple fish forms. This is the earliest representational art known in China. One bowl has two of these masks and two plain fish spaced around its interior. Around the rim are spaced four arrow-shaped marks. There must be a significance to the whole.

Bowl from Pan-p'o with ritual fish mask and fish designs.

An enormous number of painted pots have been discovered from many sites and a great deal is now known about their chronological and geographical relationships. Some of them, as at Pan-p'o, were for practical and ritual use by the living. Others were made specifically for burial with the dead. The finest of the latter are from more western sites in Kansu province, where Yangshao culture flourished in its later period. Many are painted with swirling currents of whirlwind power which defy the label of decoration. The archaeologist may sense a ritual presence, but it is beyond the reach of his science.

The burial sites of Kansu were first brought to the notice of scholars by Andersson. Unfortunately, one of the most important sites was destroyed in the process. Farmers in the Pan-shan hills occasionally dug up magnificent painted urns. They discovered that Andersson, staying seventy-five miles away to the north in Lanchow, was an eager buyer of such wares. As a consequence they dug enthusiastically and extensively for more urns, laying waste a neolithic cemetery.

Andersson had gone to Lanchow looking for evidence of Yangshao culture along the Kansu corridor. This was China's best-known route of communication with Central Asia. One site he discovered in Kansu he interpreted as earlier than the Yangshao in Central China. This of course promoted a theory that the painted-pottery culture had entered China from further west. This is now known to be wrong. Later excavations in Kansu have shown that Andersson's 'early' stage lies above Yangshao strata. Sites such as Pan-p'o have put the priority of the Wei River valley culture beyond doubt. In Kansu, also, corpses were buried curled on their side, showing a basic cultural difference from central Yangshao.

The Chinese now think of the region around the Yellow River's south-western elbow as a nuclear area. Agricultural technology in this area fostered an explosive expansion of population, forcing a migration eastwards. The eastern plains around the lower Yellow River probably became habitable only at this time. It was in this eastern region that a distinct neolithic culture was discovered by Wu Gin-ding in 1928 and excavated by Academia Sinica in 1930. The site was near the town of Lung-shan-chen, in Shantung province, and the culture has since been called the Lungshan. The most striking feature is its black pottery. This ware, unlike that of the Yangshao, was made on a wheel and its thin-walled black body is polished to shining smoothness. The finest pieces are undecorated, save for a few incised lines. The remarkable shapes, often with angular contours, and straight or even concave sides, look more suited to metal rather than clay. But it is not a metal-using culture.

Lungshan settlements were more permanent than those of the Yangshao. Their crops were more varied and included rice. They husbanded more animals, including cattle and sheep. They raised their settlements on earthen mounds to defend increasingly complex communities. A greater occurrence of offensive stone weapons shows the growth of warfare between neighbouring villages.

For thirty years the Lungshan culture was thought to be distinct from the Yangshao in both nature and origin. But in 1956 and 1957 this view was radically changed by excavations at Miao-ti-kou, between Yang-shao-ts'un and Pan-p'o. The sequence here convinced Chinese archaeologists that in fact the Lungshan had developed directly out of the Yangshao. The crucial stage occurred in north-western Honan, but it fully matured further east. Related developments have been found further west and also far into south-eastern China, down the coast and along the Yangtze River. At the southern limit the Nanling Mountains raised a barrier between these developments and the Bacsonian culture of Indo-China.

North-eastern Honan is where China's Bronze Age appears during the Shang dynasty, starting about the sixteenth century BC. Several features of the Lungshan culture, such as foundations of pounded earth, the heating of bones for consulting an oracle and societal differentiation in the settlement pattern, clearly foreshadow the Shang. A continuity between the two has been shown at several sites. The theory of continuity between the Yangshao and the Lungshan therefore entails a most important conclusion. China has an unbroken cultural continuum from the earliest Neolithic, through the Bronze Age and down to the present. Although this thesis has been persuasively argued, there are peculiarities of the Lungshan which still lead some to question it. In the Lungshan stage, for example, the practice of burying corpses with head to the east predominated in the east and spread westwards, as far as Yang-shao-ts'un itself. Vessel forms, such as the tripod, and ritual objects, such as jade rings, are also particularly distinct. Archaeology still has many questions to answer about the relationship between the Yangshao and the Lungshan.

Black pottery beaker from the Lungshan culture in Shantung. These highly polished vessels were turned on a potter's wheel.

45

4

The Oracle of Shang

The Shang dynasty, flourishing in the second millennium BC, enjoyed an eminent place in Chinese historical writings down to the present century. Fifty years ago many people had decided that the Shang was a myth. Nowadays it is thought of as one of the most important periods in China's history: her Bronze Age and the earliest known phase of her literate civilisation. The story of its rejection and rediscovery is a fascinating one. It brought to light the most important archaeological site in China, the excavation of which has moulded today's leading generation of Chinese archaeologists and continues to train that of tomorrow. It was the ground on which the confrontation between traditional and modern historiography first reached a major resolution. To appreciate the peculiar impact of archaeology in this event, we must first understand how Chinese historians have viewed the Shang over the centuries.

The study of history is one of China's oldest and most revered traditions. Confucius himself thought that his fame would depend on his compilation of the *Spring and Autumn Annals*, a record of events concerning Confucius' native state and perhaps the earliest Chinese historical work to survive. In the first century BC, one of the world's most remarkable studies of history was written by a Grand Historian at the Han emperor's court. This man, Ssu-ma Ch'ien, was one of his nation's most travelled scholars and had one of its most critical minds. He was of such unbending integrity that his wrathfully intolerant emperor was at one moment provoked into ordering his castration. Despite this shattering tragedy, he completed a history of unprecedented scope and discipline. This *Records of the Historian* is estimated as being equivalent in length to 1,500,000 words of English.

Ssu-ma Ch'ien's work had been made both more difficult and more vital by the ruthless Emperor of Ch'in, who had achieved a military unification of China a hundred and twenty years before. Fearing intellectual dissent, this ruler had attempted to destroy every book in the land. Ssu-ma Ch'ien had therefore to start on a great labour of reconstruction. His work has remained to the present day one of the chief sources for knowledge of China before the Han dynasty. Relating the origins of the Chinese people, he started with a succession of legendary emperors, followed by the Three Dynasties of Hsia, Shang and Chou. This epoch had been finally destroyed by the Emperor of Ch'in. Although it is only with the ninth century BC, during the Chou dynasty, that Ssu-ma Ch'ien considered his dating beyond question, he gives not a little information about the Shang, including the genealogy of their kings.

Ssu-ma Ch'ien's researches throughout the Empire were so thorough that he has been called China's first archaeologist. Ironically, the influence of his *Records* was so great that such on-the-spot observation rarely entered into the subsequent writing of official history. The *Records* were cast in the mould of Confucian idealistic history. The Shang were important because they were part of the Golden Age of the Three Dynasties, not because of any material developments in their culture. There was another Han dynasty historian, Yuan K'ang, who wrote that, in the age of the legendary emperors, implements were made of stone; in the Hsia dynasty, implements were made of bronze; in the Chou dynasty they were made of iron. But it was nearly two thousand years before such a scientific view of history was developed further, or even recalled.

Information about the Shang is contained in a number of other works. The most interesting is the *Bamboo Annals*, so-called because it was written on slips of bamboo, buried in a prince's tomb in 295 BC and then discovered in 281 AD, when books were no longer made in this way. Its discovery caused great excitement, because it was written in the old, pre-Han annalistic form and because it physically pre-dated the Ch'in destruction. Unfortunately its text subsequently became extremely corrupt and the modern version is an attempted reconstruction. It differs in some matters, such as the dates of the Shang, from Ssu-ma Ch'ien and other authorities. Modern Chinese scholars favour dates derived from the *Bamboo Annals*, and we follow them in this book.

After these *Annals*, documentation of the ancient period significantly increased in only one way. From an early date bronze vessels were associated with the Three Dynasties. The founder of the Hsia was supposed to have symbolised authority over the nine divisions of the Empire by casting nine bronze tripods. Han dynasty emperors made repeated attempts to recover them. The re-appearance of any ancient vessel at this time was thought to be an auspicious portent. Much later, in the Sung dynasty, there was great antiquarian interest in such relics. The ancient bronzes often bore inscriptions and these, rather than the vessels themselves, were the true object of interest. Much information about the Chou was gleaned in this way. Some inscriptions, usually very brief, were engraved in a script very different from current Chinese characters and vividly pictographic. Some of these were deciphered, but no information was extracted from them. Vessels so inscribed were attributed to the Hsia and Shang dynasties. The study of these inscriptions became particularly popular in the eighteenth and nineteenth centuries.

The agonising compulsion to reform which tightened its grip on China during the nineteenth century affected equally her views of the future and of the past. In the upheavals accompanying the republican revolution in 1911, many intellectuals felt that the enduring and worthwhile elements of Chinese civilisation could only be uncovered by a searchingly critical re-examination. Several leading historians were among these reformers. Faced with the formidable array of China's traditional historians, they raised the slogan 'Show your proof!' In an epochal collection of studies, published in the 1920s, they banished the Shang and Hsia into mythology. They even doubted the reality of the Chou, the age of Confucius himself.

As it happened, there was already an answer to some of these doubts, but the evidence was not readily accepted. It had begun to form in 1889, when an unconventional scholar, Liu E, came to Peking to visit a sick friend, Wang I-jung. He found Wang preparing a medicinal dose and noticed that one ingredient, a piece of ancient tortoise-shell, had faintly visible marks scratched on its surface. They looked hard at these marks and became convinced that they were a form of script, but so ancient as to be indecipherable. Growing curiosity led them to Wang's apothecary.

The apothecaries of Peking were well acquainted with these objects. They were coming from a village called Hsiao-t'un, near the town of Anyang in northern Honan province. When heavy rains or frost broke the earth, they were constantly churned up by the farmers' ploughs. They had been a nuisance for years. Bones and shells of strange and ancient form were often called 'dragon bones'. Dragons played a

Characters cast on a Shang bronze vessel, possibly clan names. Two eyes over a tiger flanked by bundles of record slips.

Augural inscription on
ox scapula from
Anyang.

prominent and often auspicious role in Chinese folk-lore. They were
believed to shed bones as they grew and these, when found, were
ground into medicinal powder. The farmers realised this and turned
an extra copper or two for every pound of bones delivered to apothecaries in Anyang. Frequently these bones had signs scratched on
their surface, which was not a proper attribute of dragon bones. The
farmers would therefore hack such signs off with a spade, or throw
the unwanted piece into a dry well.

49

The interest of Liu and Wang roused an antique dealer, who hurried to Hsiao-t'un. There he amazed the local farmers by offering to buy only the bones with signs—at a rate of two and a half silver pieces for every sign. Wang I-jung, with faint suspicions about the true nature of the discovery, collected eagerly and bought 912 pieces of both bone and tortoise-shell from the dealer. Then, in August 1900, Peking was thrown into turmoil by peasant rebel forces besieging the hated Westerners in their residential quarter. The siege was lifted by an Allied Relief Expedition. Wang I-jung felt so deeply the humiliation of his country that he committed suicide, leaving a destitute son with a collection of apparently useless bones. Fortunately, Liu E had shared Wang's suspicions but not his patriotic scruples. He bought the collection and began to enlarge it.

Liu died in banishment in 1908, having run foul of the most powerful art collector in the country. But in 1903 he had selected over a thousand pieces of bone and shell and published them. Using a Chinese dictionary compiled two thousand years before, he had attempted to decipher the signs. But he had been forced to admit almost total failure, except in one tantalising respect. He had recognised a group of characters used in the Chinese calendar. One of the earliest known usages of these characters was a very peculiar one; they had been used to name the kings of the Shang.

It was thus that the modern age first recognised a contemporary Shang document. Liu E's publication had been seen by one Sun I-jang, an epigraphic scholar of great ability. Applying his knowledge of ancient bronze inscriptions, in 1904 he published the results of a few months' intense study. The 'dragon bones' were no less than bones used by the Shang royal clan in consulting their oracles, inscribed with a record of the augury. Sun wrote in his preface: 'I never dreamed that in my old age I should see such treasure!'

He and a very few friends were alone in paying any attention. They were immensely learned students of their own civilisation. For thousands of years scholars had laboured in its interpretation, often reaching new insights on an intellectual and philosophical level; rarely expecting, still less finding, new material evidence. They were never exposed to the revelations of hitherto unsuspected horizons, to which archaeology has nowadays so accustomed us. For them, the sudden contact with the significance of the bones, a live transmission direct from the oracle of Shang, was a truly stunning experience.

Sun I-jang's work marked the beginning of a new learning in China, *chia-ku-hsueh*, the 'study of tortoise-shell and bone'. For the

Chinese it is a branch of archaeology peculiar to their tradition. Sun also opened a new era for the farmers of Hsiao-t'un, and within a few months scholars and collectors from China, Japan and the West were bringing the market to their front door. Yet barely a ripple was felt over the broader seas of learning, probably because the times threatened other more furious storms. Liu E had been helped in preparing rubbings of his collection by a certain Lo Chen-yü. Lo, although he had become formidably learned, was a quiet and modest man. For ten years he waited for the importance of the oracle-bones to be recognised, and waited in vain. Finally he resolved it to be his own duty and threw himself completely into the task. Often he forgot both sleep and food, struggling for days on end with a single character, searching in the darkness of a civilisation unexplored for three thousand years. After 'locking myself in my room for forty days' he completed his major contribution in 1914. A study of the content of the inscriptions, it had seven chapters: on the Shang capital; Kings and royal ancestors; Names of persons; Geographical names; Ritual institutions; Purposes of divination and Methods of divination. Few had suspected such a rich harvest.

Characters cast on a Shang bronze vessel. A great man surrounded by two horses and a boar over an honorific title.

Lo Chen-yü had an assistant, Wang Kuo-wei, a brilliant young man who was later to reconstruct the *Bamboo Annals*. Wang became obsessed with the recurrence throughout the inscriptions of the phrase *Wang-hai*. Through a painstaking process of relating the inscriptions to traditional documents, he found that *Wang-hai* was none other than the Ancestral God of the Shang, referred to by other names in later texts. In 1917 he published a study of immense importance on the Shang kings and their ancestors. From the inscriptions that recorded oracular consultations with these ancestors, he reconstructed the succession of Shang kings and provided a dramatic vindication of the king-lists preserved over thousands of years by Ssu-ma Ch'ien's *Records*. Despite a few subsequent modifications to the lists of both Wang and Ssu-ma, the former's research provided the first substantial proof that the latter not only had recorded an authentic civilisation, but had done so accurately.

This was the answer to the sceptical historians who thought the Shang a myth. By this time the farmers of Hsiao-t'un, between the rotation of wheat and millet, had harvested a crop of some 80,000 pieces of oracle-bone. But the oracle-inscriptions were still dismissed as misinterpretation or forgery, or simply ignored. In 1928 Academia Sinica was founded as China's first institute of scientific research.

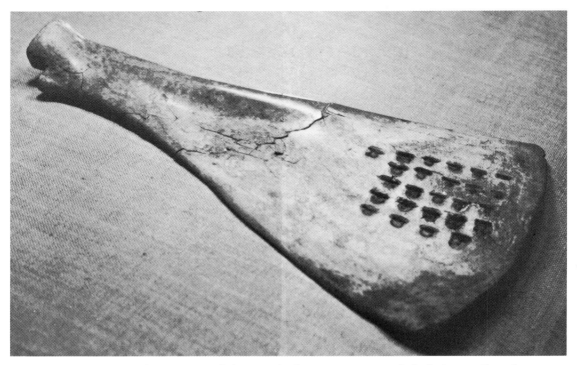

Early Shang oracle-bone from Chengchow. A heated instrument has been applied to drilled cavities: the augural queries are on the reverse side of the scapula.

The source of the oracle-bones was one of their immediate interests and in the same year they sent a man to investigate the village of Hsiao-t'un. Thus did a search for oracle-bones, an obscure pursuit of a peculiarly Chinese piece of history, result in the finding of the Great City of Shang, one of the world's most important archaeological excavations. The story of these excavations will be told in the next chapter. Here we are concerned with their effect on studies of the Shang oracle. The man sent by Academia Sinica to Hsiao-t'un was Tung Tso-pin, who by the time he died in 1963 had long been acknowledged as the world's greatest authority on the oracle-bones. He played a leading role in the pre-war excavations at Hsiao-t'un, during which a total of 28,574 pieces of oracle-bone was found. 1928 marked a watershed. From this time the sceptics' demand to 'Show your proof' was incontrovertibly answered.

The finds showed that the diviners used ox scapula and femur, and tortoise carapace and plastron. Each piece could be used for many divinations. At a chosen spot on the under-face of the bone or shell they drilled a small oval depression, to which they then applied a heated point. The bone cracked and from the fissures was divined the oracle's answer. The pattern of fissures was usually one long line and a shorter branching off it. Reflecting this, the character *pu*, 'to divine', is still written ⎰. Sometimes the diviners inscribed their question or the answer, or both. Occasionally they later added a comment about what actually happened. The script is not necessarily the earliest form of Chinese writing known. It is more abstract than the pictographs which appear on some Shang bronzes and it may represent a more advanced clerical script of the time.

Divining was a royal practice, although recent discoveries have shown its occurrence in other important households. The questions concerned many aspects of the royal house, such as sickness and birth, travel and hunting. From the reign of King Wu-ting comes this:

'Divine on the day *wu-wu*. Ku divined.
We are going to hunt at Ch'iu. Any capture?
The hunt on this day actually captured 1 tiger, 40 deer, 164 foxes, 159 hornless deer . . .'

Questions of wider significance often dealt with military expeditions and agriculture. Especially frequent were questions of fortune and weather during the coming days. For example:

'Divine on the day *keng-tzu*. Cheng divined.
Tomorrow, will the weather be fine, or not?
The king read the signs and said: This evening it will rain, tomorrow it will be fine.
In that night rain was given. On the morrow it was fine.'

In this instance the king himself read the answer, a role which was favoured by the last two kings of Shang. The questions were addressed to many ears; those of the Ancestral God, preceding royal ancestors, divinities of the sun and moon and the rain and wind among others. The practice of divining probably arose out of a desire to keep in contact with ancestors of the clan, from whom guidance and authority were drawn. The ancestor cult, involving a concept of lineage, is a development which can be seen in late neolithic cemetery patterns.

The content and number of the inscriptions is in some cases sufficient to suggest the royal character. King Wu-ting, for instance, was extremely superstitious and kept his diviners busy consulting on everything from military expeditions to royal toothache. History describes him as a powerful military leader who greatly expanded Shang influence. Inscriptions bear this out by many references to the subjugation of tribes on the Shang borders. A tortoise plastron inscribed in his reign appears to have come from the region of the Malay peninsula, presumably as tribute. The commonest queries of

The character *chih*, 'to hold': *From left to right*, the script on a Shang bronze, on an oracle-bone, and the modern Chinese.

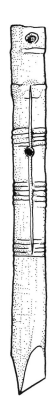

Jade knife for engraving oracle-bones, found in the royal tomb at Wu-kuan-ts'un.

his diviners are those concerning hunting. Ssu-ma Ch'ien wrote of him, 'hunting in grounds between the Yellow and Yi Rivers, he was killed by a thunderbolt.'

The excavations uncovered oracle-bones which had been carefully stored over a period of several reigns. Evidently, oracle-bones used away from the ceremonial centre, such as on a hunting trip, were brought back for central storage. An exception was found in 1934, when Tung Tso-pin went to investigate a report that villagers had uncovered a deposit in nearby Hou-chia-chuang. He discovered six complete tortoise plastrons covered with inscriptions, one of his most important finds. The plastrons had been carefully stacked together and were probably a temporary store which had been forgotten in a subsidiary palace.

Oracle-bones were also dumped *en masse*, for reasons which are still unknown. It is not clear whether one particularly dramatic example has any general significance. In 1936, in the central excavation area, a pit was found containing 17,096 pieces of oracle-bone and shell. This record cache included two hundred whole plastrons and clearance of the pit extended that season of excavation well into the dog-days of summer. The deposit in this pit, numbered H127, was much higher on one side, obviously because the contents had simply been poured in. Half-buried among them was a skeleton, crouched head-down as though hurled into the pit. Perhaps this was the diviner, buried with his store following some disaster or malpractice.

Tung Tso-pin was on the site in the excavating seasons and studying the inscriptions in between. The remarkable results of his research often affected the interpretation of the excavations, and the converse was equally true. His eye, trained to great sensitivity in the forms of handwriting, noticed consistent variations in inscriptions. His mind was intrigued by a group of characters which often came between the date of the augury and the words *pu-chen*, meaning 'divined.' Earlier students had declared these characters insoluble. Eye and mind working together, Tung realised that variations of the script tied in with variations of the mysterious characters. Hence he found that the characters were in fact the names of the diviners, and was able to work out a relative chronology for these names and to identify the personal hand of each. Over 120 of these diviners are now known. A very large number of oracle inscriptions, formerly undatable, could be located in Tung's chronology. Where such inscriptions were associated with a particular excavation, the chronology could often be applied to the site.

Shang oracle inscriptions from the reign of King Wu-ting, thirteenth century BC. On this plastron from the great hoard in pit H127 the inscription reads symmetrically out from the centre and records the diviner Wei asking about the coming harvest.

Continuing to work on the same problem, Tung found that differences in script also tied in with different formulations of the augury. Where these formulations differed from one reign to another, a division by generation was often meaningless. The twenty-second king, Wu-ting, was succeeded by his eldest son Tsu-keng, who was in turn succeeded by a younger son, Tsu-chia. The calendrical and augural practices of Tsu-keng repeated those of his father, but those of Tsu-chia were quite different, being more systematic and far simpler. Tung recalled a contradiction in traditional documents.

Whilst Ssu-ma Ch'ien had written that 'Tsu-chia was lascivious and the Shang declined further', another source praised him as one of the 'wise kings of Shang'. Tung also recalled that the adjective used by Ssu-ma Ch'ien, usually meaning 'lascivious', was explained in another text as 'opposing the dead king's institutions'. So he uncovered a great division between reactionary and reformist rulers in the Shang, both reflected and disguised in traditional histories. He interpreted this as a struggle for power, but later studies suggest that it related to a systematised alternation of rule between two main lineages of the royal clan, which had each developed their own ceremonial practices. This theory provides an explanation for the east/west division seen in structures excavated at Hsiao-t'un and other phenomena of the Shang that appear to fall into two main groups, such as the decoration of ritual vessels.

Confucius himself said of the Shang: 'How can we talk about their ritual? There is a lack of both documents and learned men!' The oracle-bones and their excavation, and the work of archaeologists such as Tung Tso-pin have now overstepped Confucius himself. But Tung acknowledged the great limitation of oracle-bone studies. They tell us virtually nothing of the Shang beyond the royal sphere and no more about some aspects, such as the bronze culture, within the royal sphere itself. Such a limitation, of course, had been characteristic of the entire Confucian tradition. The balance was partially redressed by other discoveries of the excavations near Anyang.

5

The Great City of Shang: the Bronze Age

The Hsiao-t'un district, for many years the source of Shang dynasty oracle-bones, had an ancient name, the Wastes of Yin. Yin was the name by which the Shang were called by their Chou conquerors, and both Ssu-ma Ch'ien and the *Bamboo Annals* located a late capital of the Shang in the district. Bronze vessels were said to have been looted from nearby tombs. But these implications carried little weight in 1928, when Academia Sinica sent Tung Tso-pin to investigate the area. Tung's trip fell between hyper-critical scholars who rejected the evidence as hearsay, and hyper-conservatives who felt that excavation was nothing more than irreverent and irrelevant grave-grubbing.

Tung's own search was for oracle-bones. When he reached the village, the local inhabitants came crowding around with fragments of bone for sale. He met with the village headman and discovered that bones were still being found. This was an exciting re-assurance, for even the believers like himself feared that the farmers might have long since cleared the ground of every ancient relic. He left without delay to see the President of Academia Sinica and to make plans. Funds were raised, technicians were hired, and on October 7th, Tung Tso-pin was back in Anyang with six colleagues to open the first official excavation, the first of fifteen to be conducted between 1928 and 1937.

The team began field work on October 13th. Though few and hastily assembled, they were acutely conscious of where they stood, between the ancient tradition and modern science. Tung planned to locate the centre of the site, which he thought to be north of the village. He hired the labour of fifteen farmworkers and began to sink trial trenches. For nineteen days they dug, receiving no guidance from the featureless site and finding nothing but small, discarded fragments. Tung thought of the tens of thousands of oracle-bone remains which had already come from the area and felt that his systematic intentions had met with total defeat. In his own words, 'We abandoned our own logic and took advantage of the villagers' experience.'

Recent experience, he suspected, was centred in the village itself. The villagers were most tight-lipped of all about this area, but it was hard to conceal traces of digging here. He set his men to dig near the village headman's vegetable garden, where he had noticed significant disturbance. The men, he soon realised, were reluctant to dig very deeply. Tung's probing enquiries revealed that earlier that year, when fighting between bandits and government forces had ruined the crops, the farmers had turned to digging for oracle-bones and had made a great find just where the main road skirted the headman's garden. Tung concentrated his efforts here for the remaining seven days. The trench, the thirty-sixth dug by his team, carved its way right across the road. The first five feet down were through soil already disturbed by the villagers. Below this was hard, yellowish soil, not the ashy layer for which Tung had been searching. But it yielded the inscribed bones in the cause of which Tung's life was directed: 135 inscribed pieces were discovered, together with 175 uninscribed pieces.

The work was urgent. Winter was rapidly encroaching. So also were bandits, making repeated kidnapping raids in the vicinity. The team's military guard were terrified. Tung Tso-pin, finally reassured by material success, nevertheless realised that the difficulties of the site had frustrated all theoretical plans and that the entire project needed careful rethinking. On October 30th they withdrew for the season. The nature of the site was still almost a total mystery. But an implicit message of the oracle was becoming apparent, 'Look here for the Great City of Shang.'

In December of that year, Academia Sinica established a department of archaeology. At its head was Li Chi, who had previously excavated a Yangshao site and been the first field director at Chou-kou-tien. In the spring and fall of 1929 two expeditions were made, with the main purpose of surveying the topography and stratigraphy of the site near Anyang. A properly thought-out plan, although limited in object, began to reap an increasingly rich harvest. Amongst thousands of pieces of oracle-bone were four almost complete tortoise plastrons, the first seen in this condition. Other objects, of

Bronze cooking pot of the Shang dynasty, twelfth century BC. Found in Hunan province, it shows how far south Shang influence had spread.

pottery, bronze and bone, began to appear.

In 1930, due to a dispute with the provincial authorities, Academia Sinica carried out no excavations near Anyang. Instead, they investigated the newly discovered neolithic culture at Lung-shan in Shantung province. This proved to be a much better training ground for the archaeological team. When they returned to Anyang in 1931 it was the fourth expedition but, in their own estimation, the first time that they reached the level of scientific archaeology. The team of sixteen, under Li Chi, included several men who were to become China's leading archaeologists. Proceeding on a systematic division of the Hsiao-t'un area into five sectors, they began to reveal the pattern of the site as an integral whole.

59

The fourth excavation in 1931 and those following revealed a major complex of building foundations. Many circular and quadri-lateral pits were found. Similar to those found at Yangshao sites, but deeper and much larger, they were the houses of farming and working communities. Together with stone tools, they showed that the Shang populace was still largely neolithic. But the ruling class, it became clear, used bronze—and the class division was enormous. Just north of Hsiao-t'un village, close to the river bank, extensive foundations of pounded earth were uncovered. These had been made by pounding to hardness successive thin layers of earth. These layers, on which the imprint of the pounding hammer is often still visible, are up to thirty in number and form platforms up to ten feet in depth. The largest was a full 280 feet (85 metres) long and $47\frac{1}{2}$ feet (14·5 metres) wide. It must have absorbed an immense amount of labour. On these foundations many traces of pillar bases were found. Pillars appear to have stood on great boulders sunk in the pounded earth and their spacing shows that the roof was raised on the same beam-and-upright trabeated system that was typical of Chinese architecture down to the modern age. In contrast to the flat landscape and largely sub-terranean dwellings of the common people, such edifices must have been surprisingly imposing.

It emerged that there were three major building complexes, all aligned along a north-south axis. The northernmost complex of six large and nine smaller rectangular buildings was probably the dwellings of the royal clan. The humble pit-houses of retainers and workers are clustered nearby. The differentiation of a ruling clan is one of the most important phenomena of Shang times, fundamentally changed from the egalitarian community structure of Yangshao society. Startling and gruesome evidence of their tyrannical power was found in the sector south of the royal household. The two sectors are separated by a square platform pounded from pure loess and un-marked by any traces of superstructure, which has been interpreted as a ceremonial altar. South of it lie three groups of the largest foundations discovered. They were surrounded on the east side by the burials of no fewer that 852 people, fifteen horses and five chariots, ten oxen, eighteen sheep and thirty-five dogs. All these lives had undoubtedly been sacrificed in consecration of the buildings, which are now thought to be the royal temples. The east side of this com-plex has been eroded by the river. Originally there may have been two rows of temples facing each other, representing the two main lineages of the royal clan. Slightly to the south-west of the temple complex

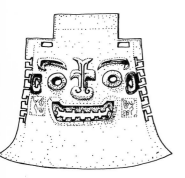

Sacrificial executioner's axe-head. One of a pair buried with the victims in a Shang tomb in Shantung.

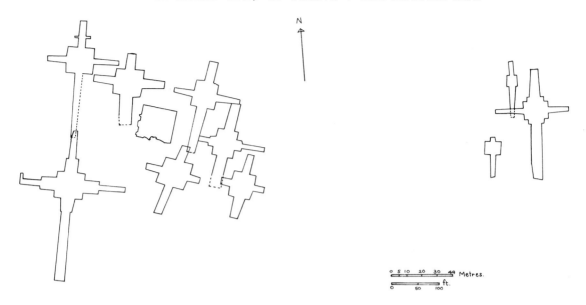

N

0 5 10 20 30 40 Metres.
0 50 100 ft.

Distribution of Shang tombs into eastern and western groups north of the river near Anyang. The square in the western group is a false tomb, and the Wu-kuan-ts'un tomb in the east is not shown.

was another, much smaller but even more systematic in pattern. This, it is thought, was the ceremonial quarter. There was an enormous concentration of oracle-bones here, including pit number H127, which contained 17,096 pieces. These foundations also were consecrated with human blood.

The oracle-bones refer many times to great sacrifices of war-captives to the royal ancestors. Just north of the river are many scattered burials of slaughtered men, which may well be those to which the diviners refer. The most impressive Shang remains were discovered near these burials. The tenth excavation, in spring 1934, moved its entire resources across the river to the village of Hsi-pei-kang, since it was said that the villagers had been looting tombs nearby. The excavators little realised that they were about to discover the Shang royal cemetery. One after another, ten great tombs of kings and one false tomb were found. In 1950, when excavations were resumed by the Communist government, an eleventh great tomb was found.

According to the king-lists, twelve kings ruled at the last Shang capital. Since the last king was said to have burnt to death in his palace, when the Chou annihilated the Shang in 1027 BC, eleven tombs is just the number we would expect. Equally suggestive is the way in which the tombs are ordered in an eastern and western group. This, like a similar ordering of the ancestral temples, is exactly what we would expect of a dual-lineage ruling house. The tombs vary in size, the longest being 110 yards from north to south. But they all share the same basic pattern of a deep squarish pit with access ramps leading into the sides. All but three have four ramps, making a characteristic cruciform plan. They all are aligned slightly east, and the southern ramp is always the longest. The tomb excavated near Wu-kuan-ts'un in 1950, which falls in with the eastern group, is an excellent example. Like all the royal tombs, it had been plundered, but its shape was intact, and the excavators were able to describe the process of its construction with some confidence.

When the king died, a great pit was marked out, 45½ feet (14 metres) long and 39 feet (12 metres) wide. The earth from its excavation was brought out along two ramps, cut progressively into the northern and southern sides. In later burial custom the southern side had ritual priority. This must have been so even in Shang times, for when the pit was nearly 15 feet (4·7 metres) deep, the northern ramp was no longer used. With access from the south the pit was continued to a total depth of 23 feet (7·2 metres). In the centre of its floor a small 'waist pit' was dug. This gateway to the underworld was then protected by the sacrificial burial of an armed warrior. Over his body a wooden floor to the main tomb chamber was laid. On this were placed four great beams to form a rectangle in the pit. The space between these beams and the sides of the pit was then filled with earth and pounded firm. This was repeated with a further eight sets of beams, thus building a massive wooden chamber, 8½ feet (2·5 metres) deep, surrounded by a platform of pounded earth. Presumably at this stage the king's corpse, already encoffined, was lowered into the chamber and surrounded with royal treasure. Above him the chamber was roofed with timbers, elaborately carved, inlaid and painted.

The king departed with terror in his train. On the platform of beaten earth around his chamber were laid the corpses of many compelled to follow. In the Wu-kuan-ts'un tomb twenty-four skele-

Royal tomb at
Wu-kuan-ts'un.
Horizontal dotted lines
show pounded earth.

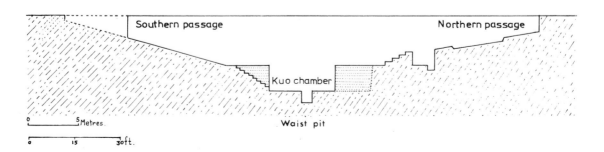

Southern passage · Northern passage · Kuo chamber · Waist pit · 0 5 Metres · 0 15 30 ft.

tons were found on the west side and seventeen on the east. They were accompanied by many objects, those on the west more ornamental and those on the east more warlike, and the skeletons must be female and male respectively. Probably they were of the king's own household, for they clearly have their own rank. The one in the centre of each side is principal, accompanied by many bronze, jade and bone objects and even a sacrificial dog. They, like some of the others, were buried in a coffin. These unfortunates must have been dispatched with care beforehand, for unlike many sacrificial burials, the corpses had been decently laid to rest.

The two entrance ramps were now protected by four dogs at the lower end of each. Higher up both ramps three pits were dug to receive sixteen horses, the ready-bridled teams for eight chariots. Between the horses squatted two armed warriors. Still the terror was inexorable, witnessed in reverse by the archaeologists. Over the array of corpses the pounding of earth began again. Many other animals, especially monkeys and deer, were buried in the process. Men were decapitated and their heads were placed in successive layers of pounded earth. Thirty-four skulls were found, all facing the centre. South of the tomb, seventeen exactly ordered subsidiary graves were located. They contained 160 headless skeletons and were unaccompanied by any objects. The connection with the skulls seems obvious and suggests that a majority of skulls has not been found. If so, at least 249 people were sacrificed to the king's after-life.

The large number of objects recovered from the Wu-kuan-ts'un tomb were mainly from the platform and ramps. Although the tomb chamber itself contained nothing but a few fragments, the largest Shang bronze vessel known, the Ssu-wu-mu quadripod weighing 13.8 cwt (700 kg), was found in a nearby field in 1939. It could well have been plundered from this tomb chamber and then abandoned. There were clear traces of at least five plundering entries, four recent but one long before. The early attempt had evidently come to a fearsome end when the wooden chamber exploded into an underground furnace, perhaps set alight by the plunderers' torch. The walls of pounded earth had been scorched to a depth of eight inches (twenty centimetres).

No unplundered royal burials have been discovered in this area, although some have still yielded very rich finds, and no oracle-bones have been discovered in these tombs. It has not therefore been possible to identify or date any of them, although there is some stratigraphical evidence which may eventually help towards a relative chronology.

OPPOSITE
Above Mortuary urn from Kansu, late Yangshao culture.
Below Tripod water pitcher from Shantung, Lungshan culture. This is not the classic black colour, but the shape is very typical of Lungshan.

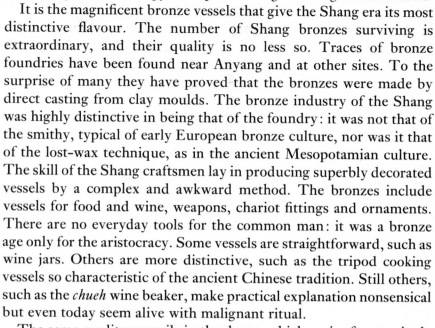

Bronze wine vessel, with *t'ao-t'ieh* mask, Shang dynasty, twelfth century BC, from Anhwei.

One of the many benefits which would accrue from this would be an archaeological chronology to help the dating of Shang bronze vessels.

It is the magnificent bronze vessels that give the Shang era its most distinctive flavour. The number of Shang bronzes surviving is extraordinary, and their quality is no less so. Traces of bronze foundries have been found near Anyang and at other sites. To the surprise of many they have proved that the bronzes were made by direct casting from clay moulds. The bronze industry of the Shang was highly distinctive in being that of the foundry: it was not that of the smithy, typical of early European bronze culture, nor was it that of the lost-wax technique, as in the ancient Mesopotamian culture. The skill of the Shang craftsmen lay in producing superbly decorated vessels by a complex and awkward method. The bronzes include vessels for food and wine, weapons, chariot fittings and ornaments. There are no everyday tools for the common man: it was a bronze age only for the aristocracy. Some vessels are straightforward, such as wine jars. Others are more distinctive, such as the tripod cooking vessels so characteristic of the ancient Chinese tradition. Still others, such as the *chueh* wine beaker, make practical explanation nonsensical but even today seem alive with malignant ritual.

The same quality prevails in the decor, which varies from a single horizontal line to fantastic metamorphoses covering an entire vessel, from vividly modelled animal heads to totally abstract schematisations. Most examples blend these aspects into a compulsive world of animal spirit. Man is but a suppliant, a small face between a monster's jaws. And always there is symmetry. Like the temples and like the tombs, everything in Shang art is symmetrical. The most perfect expression of all this is the monstrous *t'ao-t'ieh* mask decor, which appears on bronzes of all types in endless variations. Archaeology cannot penetrate these highly expressive manifestations of Shang animism, but it has already answered a hot dispute among art historians: the most simplified and highly abstracted of these masks are the earliest.

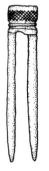

Bone hairpin, one of many found within Shang walls at Chengchow, indicating an aristocratic enclosure.

The proof of this came from Shang sites which antedate Anyang. The scale and quality of the Anyang finds became a tremendous challenge. From where had the rulers of this great city come? What explanation was there for this sudden flowering of bronze technology, so unlike any other? The first satisfactory answer came in 1950, when remains of an earlier Shang city were found under the modern city of Chengchow, just south of the Yellow River. The major feature of this site is a city wall enclosing an area of eight-tenths of a square mile

(3·2 square km.). It was made from the typically Shang layers of pounded earth and from its remains archaeologists have calculated that ten thousand men would have taken eighteen years to complete it. A very large number of elegantly carved bone hairpins have been found exclusively within its enclosure. Many oracle-bones have been found, although none are inscribed. These and several other features lead us to believe that it was the Shang capital of Ao, from whence the kings moved to Anyang in 1300 BC. Unfortunately, much of the site still lies under present occupation.

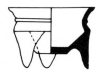

Chengchow is the earliest known city in China. There is still very little known about this important contribution of the Shang, although another city at Hui-hsien and many other smaller sites with Shang traits have been found over a wide area in Central China. Near modern Yen-shih, seventy miles west of Chengchow, a number of important sites represent the transition between Neolithic and Bronze Age. This is the area where archaeologists expect, eventually, to trace more clearly the origins of the Shang. Although the sequence from Yangshao, through Lungshan to Shang is established beyond doubt, as at the Anyang site itself, the early development of cities and their accompanying bronze technology are still largely shrouded in mystery. At Chengchow, both of these aspects are already quite advanced.

Lungshan black pottery (*above*) and Shang bronze (*below*) tripods show a marked similarity of shape.

The extraordinary speed with which the Bronze Age apparently matured in China has led some archaeologists to suggest that the technology had been introduced from further west. Chinese archaeologists vigorously oppose this suggestion, comparing it with the mistaken attempt to derive the Yangshao culture from elsewhere, and pointing to the unique characteristics of the Chinese Bronze Age. The current Chinese view of the development from Neolithic to Bronze Age admits no external influence.

However, it is hard to ignore the fact that China was comparatively late in her discovery of bronze. There are, furthermore, several peculiarities about the Lungshan-Shang cultural complex, such as the eastern concentration of the most classic Lungshan traits. In this connection it has been pointed out that North China had important links with Trans-Siberian cultures, through the valleys of the Amur and Sungari Rivers in the far north-east. This may be the most likely route by which knowledge of primitive bronze technology could have reached China. There was a very rapid transmission of such knowledge through an immense northern belt, which touched the north-eastern extent of Chinese culture. Nowadays the cold Siberian pine forests, in the second millennium BC this region was much warmer and more passable. North China itself was warmer than today—elephants were used for transport and warfare. The continuity of this contact is seen in features with Siberian connections which appear only at Anyang, in the last phase of Shang. The most interesting of these are chariots and certain forms of spears and knives. During the Shang period contact developed with pastoral tribes in a region stretching across northern China from the Ordos eastwards. This contact, through which influences ebbed and flowed, had important implications for later history.

To the west of the eastern plains lay another zone, where the earliest Yangshao sites are found and from where the Chou people expanded in their successful assault on the Shang. This area communicates with Central Asia through the Kansu corridor. In contrast, the distinctive features of Shang art and also ethnic considerations have led some to seek other connections with Pacific and South American civilisations. Such connections, if they exist, have largely eluded the archaeologist. But it is strange indeed that none of the known cultures within Shang China's continental sphere offer anything comparable to the powerful images of her art.

A Shang dynasty bronze wine container, twelfth century BC.

6

Cities and Warfare: Feudalism in the Chou Dynasty

The Shang dynasty came to an end in 1027 BC, when their rule was annihilated by the armies of the Chou. This fact alone says much about the level of Chou culture; the indications are that they were a sophisticated bronze-using people from the western region whose weaponry and technology could match that of the Shang. Yet, archaeologically speaking, our knowledge of the early Chou is meagre. Historically, they were of prime importance. The Chou dynasty lasted for nearly eight centuries (1027–256 BC), and it nurtured generations of China's greatest thinkers in many fields, forming her ideological foundations. The most influential of them was Confucius (551–479 BC) who established a school of political and ethical conduct. He was sadly disappointed in his life-long ambition to be appointed adviser to a feudal court, but his practical philosophy became immensely influential after his death.

The archaeologist may feel somewhat frustrated in the face of the wealth of information from traditional sources. For him, Confucius as a man of Chou is a virtual nonentity. But the intellectual harvest of Confucius and others was reaped from a tremendous growth in material civilisation. Much of this has come to light, in terms of agriculture and industry, cities and communications, weapons of war and objects of art. This is the archaeologist's contribution, but even so his evidence can scarcely match the reality of the civilisation.

There were hundreds of Chou cities, but very few of them have been located: the majority probably lie under the towns and cities of today. They can be excavated only occasionally, and then only in a fragmentary fashion. Beyond this limitation, it will require decades of concentrated archaeological research before a substantial and coherent material scene can match the picture drawn from traditional sources. If this ever comes about, the Chou will then emerge as a true Golden Age for the archaeologist as well as for Chinese tradition.

Little is known about the origins of the Chou. Shang oracle inscriptions clearly refer to the Chou as a tributary people in the western region, who were causing increasing trouble. Although the oracles fall silent before the moment of conquest, they do tell us that the Shang armies were engaged against tribes in the east as the Chou swept in from the west. The Chou did not have the same augural practices so we have no such record from their side. However, the Chou capital is located by tradition firmly on the banks of the Feng River, immediately south-west of modern Sian. Although this has not been doubted, nothing in the nature of a city has been revealed by extensive excavation in the area. Tradition suggests a partial reason for this, for a royal pleasure resort constructed under the T'ang is said to have destroyed some of the ancient Chou foundations.

The Feng River excavations did, however, reveal a continuum from neolithic times through to the Chou and some important burials were found. They suggest that the Chou enjoyed at least an advanced

Shang chariot burial found in 1972 south of the river near Anyang. The charioteer's skeleton can just be seen behind his chariot.

bronze technology before they conquered the Shang, although there is a major difficulty in deciding which archaeological stratum is equivalent to the time of conquest. Traditional Chinese historians, such as Ssu-ma Ch'ien, describe the Chou people as rough warriors of the hills who were miraculously transformed and matured by the responsibilities of government, and this view has been shared by several Western historians of China. Wang Kuo-wei, the brilliant student of oracle inscriptions and the *Bamboo Annals*, was one of the first to suggest that the Chou brought with them a culture that was both advanced and distinct. This is a perfect archaeological problem but it is still largely unelucidated. At an early Chou site excavated at Chang-chia-p'o on the bank of the Feng River between 1955 and 1957, one level, which has been tentatively identified as pre-conquest, produced casting moulds for bronze parts of a chariot. These indications of the technology which aided the Chou's successful offensive are supported by another Chang-chia-p'o find of seven chariot burials from a period immediately following the conquest. They were close together and were probably the cemetery of a noble clan. Four of them were excavated and of these two had not been previously plundered.

The investigation of chariot burials has become a peculiarly ingenious specialisation of Chinese archaeologists, mainly consisting of finding what is no longer there. Only a few parts of the chariots were made of bronze, such as axle-caps, linch-pins and harness fittings; the rest was of materials such as wood, which have almost invariably perished. The earlier excavations could do little more than try and relate the bronze parts, but at Chang-chia-p'o the archaeologists took advantage of the way in which decayed wood had been replaced by earth that was perceptibly darker and finer than usual— loess is particularly congenial to this phenomenon. By leaving this distinctive earth *in situ*, the excavators were left with an earthen chariot of astonishing completeness.

A very successful excavation of a Shang chariot was made near Anyang in 1972, providing a clear comparison with the early Chou chariots at Chang-chia-p'o. In both places a charioteer had been sacrificed with his horses. All the known Shang examples have a team of two horses, but the Chou burial included a team of four. The Chou chariot was also a lighter and more graceful machine. Its harness was far more elaborate, the horses' muzzles being almost covered in ropes of cowrie shells with a ferociously distinctive bronze mask between the ears. These chariots were drawn by bands which passed around the horses' girths and throats, a most inefficient method which increasingly throttled the horses the harder they pulled. For this reason four, and later even six, horses were harnessed to a single small chariot. Two horses harnessed by the throat-and-girth method can barely pull half a ton, whilst a single horse efficiently harnessed can pull a cart weighing one and a half tons. By the end of the Chou (256 BC), a much better method of harnessing had been developed, although by then the age of the military chariot had already passed. But it is worth noting that in Europe, an equivalent improvement in harness did not come until a thousand years later.

One of the great traditional figures of Chou, Sun-tzu, who wrote the *Art of War*, says that, 'Operations of war require a thousand fast four-horse chariots, a thousand four-horse covered wagons and a hundred thousand mailed infantry.' Presumably because power was

Two of the ten chariots at the Shang-ts'un-ling burial of the Crown Prince of Kuo, early seventh century BC. No human sacrifices accompanied this burial.

increasingly measured in such terms, grandiose chariot burials became a striking feature of Chou burial rites. Generally they were accompanied by the horses but not by the drivers.

One of the most successful excavations was carried out near Shang-ts'un-ling in western Honan, where three chariot burials and 234 other graves of the seventh century BC were discovered. The largest pit contained ten chariots, each with two horses. The excavators revealed with extraordinary clarity the low, latticework boxes, the gracefully upwards-curving central shafts, the straight yoke-bars and the inverted-wishbone yokes which straddled the horses' necks and carried the traces. In the right rear corner of each chariot-box is a vertical post, perhaps the fastening for a parasol or banner.

In a fourth-century burial near Hui-hsien in Honan nineteen chariots were discovered. Some of these are larger than the others and have dished wheels, with spokes slanting inwards to the hub and two strengthening struts from rim to rim across the outside. Such a sophisticated answer to the stresses suffered by a large wheel preceded by some two thousand years similar discoveries in Europe.

There is an encyclopaedia of technology called *The Artificers' Record*, which was compiled in the Han dynasty but, in the view of some scholars, contains much material from the Chou period. This view is borne out by the fascinating relationship which has developed between the text of this book and archaeological discoveries. According to its unusually practical explanations, the construction of chariot wheels was meticulously controlled and tested, while differing types of wood were carefully chosen to suit their separate parts. Excavated bronze chariot parts, such as hub fittings, fully match this level of intricacy. The Chou as a period of sophisticated technological inventiveness is a picture that is appearing with archaeological support.

The chariots buried at Chang-chia-p'o are unmistakably war chariots. Later examples, especially those near Hui-hsien, are without military accoutrements and obviously reflect the widespread use of the chariot for civil transport. This belies an overall trend of the entire Chou period, which was an ever wider and more vicious recourse to warfare as the feudal hierarchy degenerated into a struggle for power. The tremendous prestige of the early Chou rulers had lasted through several reigns, during which a vast network of local domains had been established in a hierarchy that welded together state ceremony and the royal clan.

These ceremonies were often recorded by inscriptions on bronze vessels, sometimes several hundred characters in length. This use

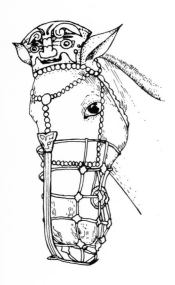

Reconstructed horse's bridle with bronze mask from early Western Chou chariot burial at Chang-chia-p'o.

of bronze vessels was a fundamental change from the ritualistic practice of the Shang. Where excavations have discovered bronzes recording occasions such as the award of a fief, Chou archaeology has gained some of its most vauluable documents.

A good example of this is the find made in 1954 of thirteen bronze vessels at Yen-tun-shan in Kiangsu province, nearly five hundred miles east of Chang-chia-p'o. One of these vessels, a somewhat inelegant *kuei* bowl, has an inscription of a hundred and twenty characters on its inside surface, which identifies its owner as a man already well-known through Ssu-ma Ch'ien's *Records*. This was the Marquis Nieh of Yi. According to the inscription, he accompanied King Ch'eng of Chou on an expedition eastwards, deep into the southern reaches of Shang. To mark this successful foray against the Shang borders, the King appointed him on the field as Marquis of Yi, which was the district around Yen-tun-shan itself. Then the King, presumably after leaving him in control of the newly occupied territory, returned to the capital with most of his army.

But such regional lords inevitably sought to stretch the limits which the system imposed on their power. When the Chou court finally succumbed to attacks by the tribes to their west and moved to their eastern capital at Loyang, in 771, their central authority began to crumble. There was no space left to absorb the territorial ambitions of regional lords and, out of about a hundred and seventy feudal domains, ten began to dominate the scene.

The cemetery at Shang-ts'un-ling affords an excellent example of this situation. The tomb associated with the pit of ten chariots contained over nine hundred items, and two weapons amongst these were inscribed, 'Dagger-axe of Crown Prince Yuan-t'u of Kuo'. The state of Kuo is clearly recorded by Ssu-ma Ch'ien as flourishing for a century after the move of the Chou capital, only to be wiped out in 655 BC by a much more powerful neighbour, the state of Chin.

We can trace these developments as they intensified through the centuries. In 1955 the tomb of a Marquis of Ts'ai was discovered near Shou-hsien in Anhwei. This is the locality where, in 447, the small domain of Ts'ai was crushed to extinction in a struggle between its two giant neighbours, the states of Ch'u and Wu. Twenty-two bronze inscriptions came from this tomb and they told a sad tale of how the Marquis had fluctuated between support for the King of Ch'u and a marriage alliance with the King of Wu.

The last two centuries of nominal Chou rule are known as the 'Warring States Era' (402–221 BC), because they were dominated

Bronze vase from the tomb of the Marquis of Ts'ai at Shou-hsien, early fifth century BC. This is a fine example of the Huai valley style of bronze casting.

by these furious conflicts, in which the code of military honour was largely extinguished. Earlier confrontations had often been resolved by a chariot duel between captains selected from the opposing forces, but now these armies battled for mass extermination. Near Hui-hsien is a common burial of sixty headless skeletons, many with arrowheads lodged in their bones. It is thought that this is a tiny relic of a great victory by the armies of Ch'in in 290. The Ch'in, eventually conquerors of all China, are reputed to have decapitated defeated enemies by the thousand.

The weaponry of these times is obviously of great interest to the archaeologist, and it is interesting to find how conservative it was in some respects. The most characteristic weapon is the *ko* dagger-axe. This is essentially a short, pointed blade mounted at a right-angle to its long handle. Those belonging to the Crown Prince Yuan-t'u of Kuo are typical of the middle Chou period, with a long tang for firm attachment to the haft. In combat, the weapon's first strike must have been a sideways swing to drive the point home, followed by a slashing pull. An extension of the blade downwards along the hafting tang greatly improved the damage done by the slashing pull. Excavations have shown that the handle, which could be up to eighteen feet long, was of asymmetrical cross-section. This would have promoted an important skill with this weapon, which was to keep it from twisting. It must have been quite effective against chariots. As the states warred ever more fiercely, increasingly fearsome variations of the *ko* were devised, adding a spear to the tip, a hooked blade behind and even a further hooked blade to the butt.

The other main hand-weapon was the sword, which was restricted to the higher ranks. The classic Eastern Chou sword, with blade and disc-terminal handle cast in one piece, was thought until recently to have been unknown earlier; but the excavations at Shang-ts'un-ling and Chang-chia-p'o have carried it back to the early Chou.

The third important arm was the bow and arrow, which had been used since Yangshao (neolithic) times. The Shang bow was a powerful reflex design. A Chou bow of the fourth century BC, excavated near Ch'ang-sha, is a reflex bow of compound construction, with four strips of bamboo bound tightly with silk, tipped with horn and fifty-five inches in length. The Shang-ts'un-ling finds showed that a sleek, three-bladed bronze arrow head was in use by the seventh century, pronged for fitting into bamboo—the perfect arrow shaft.

But the really significant advance in the development of this area of weaponry was the invention of the crossbow during the early Warring States Era. Like the conventional bow, it was made of laminated bamboo. The trigger mechanism was a strong and simple assembly of four bronze parts. The crossbow, when used to best advantage at fairly short range, fires a heavy missile at high velocity through a flat trajectory. The shattering impact of the quarrel (bolt) is greater than that of a modern high-velocity rifle bullet. In addition, it is much easier to aim and fire than a conventional bow, which becomes effective only after extensive practice. Sun-tzu wrote in the *Art of War*: 'The momentum of one skilled in war is overwhelming and his attack is precisely regulated. His potential is that of a fully drawn crossbow; his timing the release of the trigger.'

The Chou dynasty also saw China's discovery of iron; but archaeology has still to discover exactly when and how. Their iron technology was as distinctive as their bronze technology, for they appear to have used both wrought and cast iron right from the beginning. (By comparison, cast iron was not known in Europe until the fourteenth century AD.) Cast iron differs in its carbon content and requires a

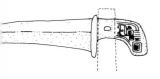

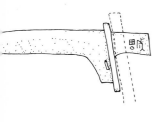

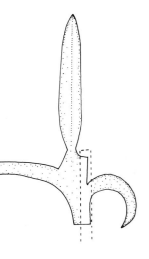

Bronze dagger-axes and their evolution from the Shang dynasty to the Warring States Era. The handles could be up to eighteen feet long.

very high temperature, about 1400°C, to reduce it from the ore; but once obtained it will melt at a lower temperature than wrought iron, and hence it can be cast in a liquid state, when wrought iron is only softened and has to be beaten into shape. Cast iron is obviously better suited to producing more complex shapes and larger quantities. Just as with the distinctiveness of China's bronze technology, a partial explanation must lie in the extraordinarily advanced development of kilns and furnaces. The great crucibles which were found in the Shang foundry site at Hsiao-t'un indicate a technology already approaching the ability to smelt cast iron.

Despite this technology, the Chinese were oddly casual in their adoption of iron. It was a long time before it was widely used for weapons. A clue is perhaps contained in an early term for iron, 'the ugly metal'. It has none of the aesthetic appeal of bronze, which went with, and was sanctioned by, an age-old ritual of forms. On the other hand, iron agricultural implements have been found in burials near Ch'ang-sha dating from the early fifth century BC, and in virtually every burial of the Warring States Era iron implements have been found. These are predominantly agricultural, such as the earliest iron ploughshare found near Hui-hsien. This represented a most important development for Chinese agriculture, for up to this time the farmer had worked with essentially Stone Age tools.

Some districts, especially in the north-west, had rich deposits of iron ore, and the associated iron foundries often became centres of a wealthy economy. Rivalry between states in the middle Chou period had been mainly over the extent of territory, but now the control of thriving cities became an increasingly important aim. Busy markets grew up in cities protected by massive walls of pounded earth. China's oldest collection of written material, the *Book of Songs*, contains a vigorous description of the building of a Chou city:

'. . . Then the duke summoned his Master of Works,
He summoned his Master of Labour
And set them to build houses.
Dead straight was the plumb line,
Lashed were the wooden frames to hold the earth,
To make the temple, venerable indeed.
They poured in the earth, rumbling,
They pounded it, thudding,
They scraped it level, clinking,
As the wall rose by feet and yards,
Even the rhythm of the drums could not keep pace . . .'

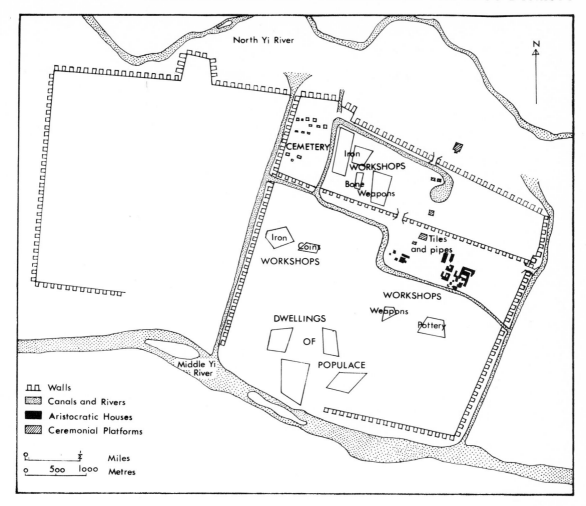

North Yi River

N

CEMETERY

Iron
WORKSHOPS
Bone
Weapons

Iron
Coins
WORKSHOPS

Tiles
and pipes

WORKSHOPS
Weapons
Pottery

DWELLINGS

OF

POPULACE

Middle Yi
River

Walls
Canals and Rivers
Aristocratic Houses
Ceremonial Platforms

0   ½   Miles
0 500 1000 Metres

Plan of excavated
features of the Warring
States city of Hsia-tu.

This is considerably more vivid than most of the excavated evidence. Although at least seventy-eight new cities are known to have been built during the Spring and Autumn Era alone, only some twenty have been actually located and none has been completely excavated. Many, such as the Eastern Chou capital of Loyang, lie under existing buildings.

The city about which most is known is that at Yi-hsien, in central Hopei. This is the site of Hsia-tu, a subsidiary capital of the state of Yen, which was occupied between 697 and 226 BC. It was first explored in 1930 and has been visited by archaeologists on several occasions since. On the last published excavation, in 1961, a number of interesting finds were made. The site lies between two branches of the Yi River, in a pass opening up to the eastern plains, and was obviously a strategic point during the Warring States Era. Now-adays a few villages cluster among flat fields, out of which rise earthen terraces and ancient hunks of wall as high as thirty feet. The walls, which are over thirty feet thick at the base, are made of pounded earth, and traces of the framing process described in the song are clearly visible. As the map shows, the walls have been traced around two adjoining squares. The western square is almost empty of cultural remains and it was probably a late extension, built to protect addi-tional population as warfare grew more rampant. The eastern square is especially well protected. Across its northern and southern face run the twin courses of the Yi River and these are connected by canals which run parallel along the eastern and western walls of the square. Two more canals once ran through the enclosure, protecting an inner area and providing transport for industrial quarters which lay nearby.

Remains scattered on these latter foundations identified workshops for iron tools, weapons, pottery, bone-carving and money. These all testify to the rapid expansion of trade in the Warring States Era, which brought about the minting of China's first money. The most common varieties, round, knife-shaped and spade-shaped coins, were all found here. Between the two internal canals a wall runs straight across from west to east, forming an innermost sanctum which must have been the aristocratic centre. Hard against the south side of this wall a great terraced platform still rises to a height of thirty-five feet and extends 430 feet in width. It once bore a palatial structure, as shown by handsomely moulded roof tiles found on top and pottery drainpipes found within. (Pottery roof tiles were an innovation of Chou builders, and the earliest known was found at Chang-chia-p'o.) To the south-east and south-west of this platform cluster the most elaborate foundations found at the site. The whole complex of platforms and terraces exhibits the strict north-south orientation which characterised Chinese city planning from the Shang to the Ch'ing dynasty. In the north-east corner is a cemetery, separated by a canal from the living and working areas. It included a large tomb mound, which is one of the earliest examples of a practice that soon became very common.

The people who lived in Hsia-tu are very shadowy figures indeed. A glimpse of them came in 1964, when a small bronze statuette was found. With a quiet, respectful face it holds up a jar in an obvious attitude of offering. In both its pose and its charming simplicity it closely resembles other figures found near Loyang. The growing skill of figurative art is one of the most attractive facets of late Chou.

Bronze figurine found at Hsia-tu, height four and a half inches.

7

Diversity and Unity: the Great Wall

An iron sword is incomparably superior to a bronze sword for slicing through one's enemy. Whether by chance or no, the first Chinese state to put the iron sword to extensive use was the one which eventually overcame all other opposition. This was the state of Ch'in, which emerged from obscure origins in the upper Wei River valley to rule the first true Chinese empire, and from which the name China derives. Both the Ch'in and the Chou, who had come from the same region centuries earlier, are often thought to be partly of non-Chinese tribal stock. During the early centuries of Chou feudal glory the Ch'in were virtually unknown, but in the year 256 BC they destroyed the vestigial Chou court and by 221 they had put down all the other semi-independent states in China. How these more aristocratic powers viewed the rude manners of the Ch'in is well shown in the remarks of a noble of Wei, who reflects exactly the sentiments of Confucius:

> 'Ch'in has the same customs as the barbarians. It has the heart of a tiger or wolf. It is avaricious, perverse, eager for profit and without sincerity. It knows nothing about etiquette and virtuous conduct and if there be any opportunity for material gain, it will disregard its relatives as if they were animals.'

Nevertheless, in 221 the pragmatic ruler of Ch'in achieved one of the most important feats in Chinese history: he brought under one central government a vast empire which stretched southwards as far as present-day Hong Kong. He also created one of the Wonders of the World—the Great Wall of China.

The history of the Warring States Era (402–221 BC) can be seen as the increasing dominance of a few major states as they devoured an

Mythological figure from a Ch'u silk manuscript, third century BC.

OPPOSITE
Jade burial suits of
Liu Sheng and his wife
Tou Wan, second
century BC.

The tomb guardian
from Hsin-yang.

erstwhile plethora of small principalities. But at the same time we are made aware of some broadly significant regional cultures: the kingdom of Ch'u in Central China, the kingdom of Tien in the south-west and the nomads in the north. This is a field in which archaeology has brought sharply into focus long-existing evidence.

The state of Ch'u was for a while the most powerful state of all. Its centre was around the great lakes through which the Yangtze passes in its middle course. This fertile, rice-growing basin connects, through the Han River, directly with the Yellow River plains. By the sixth century BC the Ch'u had developed a highly sophisticated culture with many distinct features which can be seen in their language and art.

Archaeological excavation within the Ch'u domain has mainly been of graves, and the greatest concentration of these is around the modern city of Ch'angsha. By 1960 over twelve hundred graves had been located, many of them very elaborate with carefully constructed wooden chambers. The grave-objects recovered have shown that many fine and distinctive works of metal, lacquer and wood which have been in museum collections for some decades must originally have been plundered from Ch'u graves. Metallurgy was as far advanced as it was in the north, in fact the earliest iron swords have been found in Ch'u tombs. Some weapons are inscribed with an extraordinarily curly variation of the known Chinese script of the time; it is evident that Ch'u had developed a local form of writing. This is sometimes called 'bird-script' and indeed the rhythms of bird-like arching necks, prancing legs and pluming tails are characteristic of Ch'u design, seen especially in lacquer drawing.

The wooden figurines found in many tombs, some human and others animal, show the same genius for catching a life-like gesture through fanciful exaggeration. To western eyes the most surprising objects are the monstrous, totem-like tomb guardians. One of these was found in a tomb near Hsin-yang in Honan in 1956. The tomb, under a mound, was like a six-roomed wooden house and had originally been superbly furnished with a bed, stools, a table, lutes, bells, drums, a chariot and many other smaller objects. Unfortunately it was only discovered when the local villagers were sinking a well right through its middle, so it had suffered a great deal of destruction. But in the centre rear chamber was preserved a horned guardian monster, four and a half feet high, carved from wood and brightly painted. With its blood-red tongue hanging down to its knees and its eyes like dinner-plates, a more effective guardian could hardly be

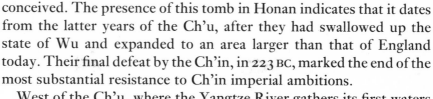

The Great Wall in Shansi province, the northern frontier of China's first empire.

conceived. The presence of this tomb in Honan indicates that it dates from the latter years of the Ch'u, after they had swallowed up the state of Wu and expanded to an area larger than that of England today. Their final defeat by the Ch'in, in 223 BC, marked the end of the most substantial resistance to Ch'in imperial ambitions.

West of the Ch'u, where the Yangtze River gathers its first waters among the smooth-faced mountains and plunging valleys of modern Yunnan province, appeared a culture with an even more individual face—the kingdom of Tien. In the Warring States Era contact was made between this region and Ch'u and the technologies of bronze, iron and irrigation seem all to have taken flourishing root together, although the route and manner of their introduction has yet to be archaeologically determined. A cemetery at Shih-chai-shan, above Lake Tien, was excavated between 1955 and 1960 and revealed a climax of this culture which astounded everybody concerned. Many of the objects are clearly related to Chinese prototypes, such as the long iron sword and bronze dagger-axe. But they are varied and decorated with a superbly vigorous skill and inventiveness. The descriptive brilliance and expressive miniature sculpting are un-matched elsewhere in China. They show prosperous farmers, cattle-raising and busy markets, hunting with dogs, ladies in sedan chairs, and shamanistic rituals with human sacrifice, and they give us much other information besides. The most elaborate enactments are on the flat lids of drum-like containers for cowries—a form of currency.

Kettle-drums found in the same cemetery provide important archaeological evidence which in fact takes the kingdom of Tien out of the Chinese cultural sphere. These drums are of the type long associated with the Dong-son culture of Indo-China. The Yunnan plateau is drained not only by the Yangtze, but also by the Red and the Mekong Rivers, which flow into the territory of the Dong-son civilisation.

This cultural sphere of South East Asia spread across into China's southernmost provinces, but was largely divided from the northerly cultures of Ch'u and beyond by the Nan-ling Mountains and south-eastern uplands. It has been suggested that Tien not only belonged to this sphere, but was in fact the source of its bronze culture. Nevertheless, Tien eventually came under Chinese political control. In a grave at Shih-chai-shan archaeologists found a gold seal, with the legend 'Seal of the King of Tien'. In 109 BC the ruler of Tien had submitted to a Chinese show of force in return for this title.

Along China's northern borders flourished another distinct

Bronze dagger from Shih-chai-shan.

81

culture, that of the nomadic tribes in the northern grasslands. The line between them and the Chinese agricultural settlements can be traced back to neolithic times. During the late Shang dynasty the region's culture was vigorous enough to make its own contributions, as seen in the knives of charioteers in sacrificial burials: the backward-curving blades and handles ending in a ring or animal head were distinctively northern features.

The activities of the northern tribes during the early centuries of the Chou are still obscure. But in this period several large tribes developed into tough, independent horse-riding powers, which constantly harrassed the northernmost farming communities of the Chinese. The Chinese states with northern borders expended much military effort in contesting these border regions. The Chin, which was the first feudal territory of the Chou to wax great and then wain, conducted at least two major campaigns against the nomads. In the eighth century BC they drove one group out of the area now called Shansi, eastwards beyond the T'ai-hang Mountains. In the seventh century BC they campaigned in the north-west, pushing another group out into the Ordos. The battles of Chinese against nomads, of alliances between Chinese and nomads against other such alliances were constant. By the late Warring States Era one tribe, the Hsiung-nu, had come to dominate the others from a central base in the Ordos. Their defeat was the last triumph of the Ch'in army, in 214. Even so, they recovered to become a major threat to the following Han dynasty and Ssu-ma Ch'ien wrote admiringly of their hardy ways.

The nomad warrior's equipment was straightforward: a sword and a bow and arrows, with small bronze buckles and plaques to ornament his belt and the harness of his horse. These bronze pieces were cast with unpretentious but vigorous designs drawn from his experience of animals, and these motifs were enthusiastically adopted by his Chinese foes. They can be seen in almost every aspect of late Chou art. A fine example of a belt plaque found *in situ* in an Eastern Chou burial at Chang-chia-p'o, shows a wrestling match between two burly warriors who have just dismounted from their horses. The commonest theme is a fight between animals, often of hunting dogs dragging down a stag. This 'animal-combat' theme was extra-ordinarily widespread, right across the nomadic civilisation of the Scyths who galloped through Asia in the sixth century. Such themes are of great interest in connection with a type of bronze vessel which becomes common in excavations of Chinese sites from the fifth century BC and later. These are the 'hunting vases,' which are

Eastern Chou bronze belt plaque showing nomad influences.

profusely decorated with scenes cast in light relief. The majority of these are of the battle and hunt and provide a vivid commentary on their times.

To cope with the nomads in the fourth century BC, the northern states started to build walls of pounded earth to protect their frontiers and the Great Wall of China was the climax of this defensive attitude. Yen, for example, protected herself in this way with a wall built around 300 BC. The walls were fairly successful, enabling the states to set up a line of well-protected garrisons. By this time the crossbow had come into use, and its compactness and accuracy over a short range made it very effective for defending a wall against nomad horsemen. The nomads stuck to their conventional bow, which was far more convenient for use on horseback, and the Chinese began to abandon the chariot in favour of cavalry, for the chariot was at a grave disadvantage in combat with the nimble nomad horsemen.

The Ch'in, in their north-western home, had as much experience of nomad attacks as had any Chinese state, and when the Ch'in ruler established himself in 221 BC as Ch'in-Shih-huang, 'First Emperor' of a Chinese empire, one of his first enterprises was to join up the various sections of earlier walls into a huge defensive rampart that snaked across the mountains for nearly three thousand miles. Much of the earlier wall was simply earth embankments, and Ch'in-Shih-huang faced these sections with stone. The present wall exists as it was restored in the Ming dynasty and is less than half the length of the Ch'in construction. Many consider that the usefulness of such a wall did not long survive the time of its original construction, but it has retained an immense symbolic importance.

83

Ch'in-Shih-huang's government was remarkable for the brilliance of its practical measures, such as unifying the script, the forms of currency and the width of carriage tracks. But his ruthless suppression of all intellectual debate—in 215 he ordered all books in the Empire to be burnt—so blackened his image in the ensuing centuries that he was ignored as an unspeakable villain rather than elevated as a national hero of unmatched achievements. His only other physical monument is his burial mound, which is located by an extensive historical tradition near the town of Lin-t'ung, a few miles due east of modern Sian. The historian Ssu-ma Ch'ien relates that he was encoffined in bronze and buried under a huge artificial hill, surrounded

Cowrie shell container from Yunnan province, second century BC.

Pottery figure found near the funeral mound of the Emperor of Ch'in.

by a sea of mercury and protected by arrow-firing booby-traps. This has been identified as the great man-made mound that can be seen to this day in the district, surrounded by the remains of an inner and outer walled enclosure which is about seven thousand yards along its greatest dimension. The mound has not yet been excavated, but four seated pottery figures have been found at various times beside the wall. They are all around two and half feet in height and are superbly modelled in attitudes of respectful servitude, which adds strength to the belief that the mound contains a royal burial. The only other objects found at the site are faint traces of buildings and part of an elaborately constructed drainage system. But such are the archaeological riches of the Sian area that it may be a long time before the mound itself will be systematically excavated.

8

The Spirit World in the Han Dynasty

The Great Wall symbolised the first unification of China. As a feat of military engineering it represented unification by the sword, and as a line of defence it held off the Hsiung-nu nomads in the north. It was no defence, however, against the enmity which raged inside the empire's borders. Within fifteen years a soldier of humble origins had buried the Ch'in triumph in obscurity under the palaces of a new dynastic glory—the Han dynasty. By a strange quirk, Westerners have come to know the land as China, derived from the name of Ch'in; but the Chinese themselves, down to the present day, proudly call themselves 'men of Han'.

The Han founder, like those of both Chou and Ch'in, came from the Wei River valley and established his capital in the Sian district. He named it Ch'ang-an, 'City of Eternal Peace', but, again like the Chou, his successors were forced to move towards the centre in Honan, and there they re-established their Eastern Capital at Loyang in 25 AD. However, during their first two centuries the Han emperors broadened their empire through military, commercial, intellectual and territorial power, which matched that of the Roman Empire. Armies of the two empires appear, in fact, to have briefly clashed in 36 BC in the area north of modern Afghanistan.

The Chou period had established China's ideological foundations; the Han formed many of the basic practical models for her society and its government. The imperial institution, which provided an enduring core to the system, took on its fundamental nature of a despotic monarchy committed to a rule of paternal benevolence and ultimately dependent upon the consent of the 'family'. The emperor's title of 'Son of Heaven' was in theory as much one of responsibility

86

An entertainment of acrobatics and dancing, with musicians and audience. The long-sleeved dance was an aristocratic tradition, the acrobatics were more proletarian. Pottery grave-model of the second century BC.

as of privilege. An outstanding example of this development was the Emperor Wu-ti, the 'Martial Emperor', who ruled from 140 to 86 BC. He indulged in megalomaniac military campaigns but he was also largely responsible for the final triumph of Confucianism among rivalling political philosophies. It was Wu-ti who had Ssu-ma Ch'ien castrated for outspoken criticism—but continued to honour him as Court Historian. Wu-ti was also a ruler of genius, who created great canal systems and nationalised the iron and salt industries.

Archaeology may eventually uncover enough evidence to shed much light on major material aspects of Han civilisation such as industry and communications. But, conversely, there are other aspects of Han life which have already greatly illuminated the archaeologists' understanding. Most intriguing among these are the fertile superstitions of the time, that inveigled men into the hope of taking with them to an afterlife the entire paraphernalia of their earthly life. Except in rare instances, the horrifyingly literal expression of these hopes, as seen in the sacrificial burials of earlier ages, was now unknown. Confucius had remarked with relief on the substitution of figurines for human victims and it was a culmination of this development which has so greatly rewarded Han archaeology.

The elaboration of Han tomb furnishings embraced not only

household treasures but reproduced the humdrum world as well. Models of people and animals fill miniature homesteads and farms; dramatic troupes entertain eternity, pigs roll in a pen shared with a saintly privy, carts and boats provide for excursions in the spirit world. The details of daily life as they are revealed by funerary figurines multiply with every excavation of a Han tomb, bringing invaluable information on architecture, clothes, mechanical engineering and many other facets of Han existence. One of the most fascinating single pieces is an acrobatic entertainment recently found in an early Western Han tomb in Shantung. The lively scene is modelled in clay on a base $26\frac{3}{8}$ by $18\frac{3}{4}$ inches (67×47.5 cm), with twenty-one figures effectively simple in form and brightly painted with colours which are still fresh. Spectators stand stiffly on either side, whilst slight and nimble dancers and acrobats perform to the accompaniment of zither, pipes, gongs and drums. These models contribute much to our knowledge on such points as the co-operation of men and women in these popular troupes, their accompaniment by music and the instruments played.

The dead with any pretensions to rank could be housed in tombs of three main forms: an elaborate wooden chamber sunk in a vertical pit and covered with a mound; a series of chambers built of great stone slabs or bricks and buried under an earthen mound; or a cave complex excavated in a hillside. Some slab-chamber tombs of the Later Han have been well-known for some decades. When first discovered, the chambers were collapsed and the slabs scattered. But many of the slabs are covered with engraved pictures, and comparison of both their shapes and their decoration resulted in a theoretical reconstruction. This showed that this type of chamber's interior was engraved with a systematic illustration of the occupant's way of life, combined with episodes of mythology and history, and contained within the diagrammatic framework of a two-storied house.

The Han emperors themselves were entombed in chambers under vast artificial hills, which were probably raised by convict labour. There have been no excavations of royal burials yet, but in 1972 an unpleasant sidelight was shed on the obsequies of Emperor Ching-ti (died 141 BC) by the discovery near his tomb of thirty-five skeletons in rough graves. Some were still wearing neck and leg irons and a few had been decapitated while thus shackled. Many such skeletons have been found here on the fringes of Ching-ti's mausoleum and they probably represent harsh treatment of convict labourers, rather than sacrificial victims. Roof tiles found within the mausoleum's enclosure

Iron collar for a convict found round the neck of a decapitated victim, probably a labourer, near the tomb of Emperor Ching-ti.

proclaim 'Joy Everlasting'.

The early Han emperors appointed their relatives to maintain the imperial presence throughout the empire in ten principalities. One of the principalities was Chung-shan, which governed a population of some 600,000 people in the region of modern Peking, and the discovery of the tombs of the first Prince of Chung-shan and his wife, Liu Sheng and Tou Wan, was one of the most exciting archaeological events of the Cultural Revolution that began in 1966.

The two burials had been made in caves cut deep into the steep sides of barren hills on the outskirts of Man-ch'eng, a town lying thirty miles south-west of the Warring States site of Hsia-tu. The discovery has been related by one of the men involved:

'In June 1968 I was on duty with a detachment of the People's Liberation Army in the Man-ch'eng district. One evening, comrades of the 12th Troop on night patrol discovered a subterranean structure and immediately reported it to Company Headquarters. When the Company Commander, Comrade Kou Chun-lin, heard the news, he leapt from his bed and drove many miles to the scene of the report. On arrival, in company with an officer he led the way down into the subterranean structure to conduct an investigation. Inside, the light of their torch could not reach the far end: it was a vast cavern, big enough to hold a thousand men, a feat of careful engineering, a veritable underground palace. The glint of gold, silver and jade everywhere met their eyes, vessels of bronze, lacquer and pottery lay row upon ordered row. On the inner face of an especially finely wrought vessel they found the words "Palace Treasure of Chung-shan", and realised that these were historical relics buried in an ancient tomb. We immediately halted the operation and made a report to our superior Party Committee. By noon the next day the Central Committee had heard the news and the Chinese Academy of Sciences sent archaeologists to our Company. A preliminary investigation revealed that it was the tomb of Liu Sheng, Prince of Chung-shan of the Former Han, dating from about 100 BC. It was decided, in order to prevent any damage to historical objects, that no one might enter the tomb without an introduction from the local political office and we mounted a guard on the hillside . . . After a great discussion, we joined forces with the local peasantry and threw ourselves into the labour of clearing and excavating the tomb . . . Comrade Kuo Mo-jo, member of the Central Committee of the CCP and an

Pottery model of a fortified house, from a general's tomb at Wu-wei, c. 170 AD.

extremely busy man, somehow found time to come to our Company and inspect this Former Han tomb for himself. He presented us with a portrait of Chairman Mao and then took up his brush to write a poem, hymning the praises of the creative wisdom of our country's workers and the treasure of her ancient art . . .'

During the excavation, rubble was noticed on an adjoining hillside, similar to the obvious traces of the original construction which still marked the entrance to Liu Sheng's tomb. This proved, indeed, to be evidence of Tou Wan's tomb, and an exploration of the area soon uncovered the entrance.

Liu Sheng was an elder brother of Emperor Wu-ti and he ruled Chung-shan for nearly forty years, dying in 113 BC. His wife died some time within the following ten years. Their tombs reflect at least some of the Han imperial splendour and the discovery created a sensation, due to the wealth of the contents. Many of the outstanding items among a total of 2,800 are unique. Liu Sheng's tomb, which must have taken well over a year to dig out, stretches 171 feet (52 metres) into the hillside. The entrance tunnel was filled with rocks and earth, its mouth was closed by two brick walls and then sealed by molten iron poured into the cavity between the walls. How this was done up on the steep hillside is hard to imagine. The tunnel leads into an ante-chamber, from which branch two long side-chambers and in these were found six carriages, the skeletons of sixteen horses and eleven dogs, a large store of food and wine, and a grind-stone complete with a horse to turn it. The ante-chamber leads directly into the central chamber, in which vessels and figurines of all descriptions were carefully laid out. These preliminary chambers had originally been lined with wooden walls and tiled roofs, and the central chamber had been hung with embroidered curtains; but these had all decayed. A drainage system ran into a well. At the far end of the central chamber a great stone portal led to the coffin chamber, lined with stone slabs and complete with a bathroom annexe. An ambulatory, opening from the central chamber, ran round the coffin chamber.

Within the coffin chambers were objects which must have been among the dead man and woman's most treasured possessions. Among those of Tou Wan was a superbly sculpted gilt-bronze lamp, inscribed 'Lamp of the Palace of Eternal Trust'. Liu Sheng and Tou Wan were cousins, and their common grandmother was an immensely powerful Empress Dowager during the reigns of the Emperors Ching-ti and Wu-ti. The Empress Dowager's residence was called

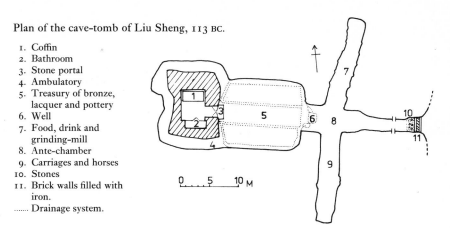

Plan of the cave-tomb of Liu Sheng, 113 BC.

1. Coffin
2. Bathroom
3. Stone portal
4. Ambulatory
5. Treasury of bronze, lacquer and pottery
6. Well
7. Food, drink and grinding-mill
8. Ante-chamber
9. Carriages and horses
10. Stones
11. Brick walls filled with iron.
.... Drainage system.

the Palace of Eternal Trust, so the lamp must have been a wedding gift to her grand-daughter. Its light-box turns smoothly to adjust the amount of light and its direction. Smoke is drawn in through the right arm so that soot is deposited within the hollow body. Several other examples of this ingenious Han design are now known.

But what has made the Man-ch'eng tombs celebrated now throughout the world are the jade suits in which Liu Sheng and Tou Wan were buried. These were each made from thousands of jade pieces, threaded together with gold to form a suit which totally enclosed the corpse. Such funeral garb was described by Han writers as an extravagance of nobles and a number of fragmentary examples have been found, but these are the first complete examples. We know that there were three official grades for such suits, and that they were sewn together with gold, silver or bronze thread. Gold thread was an imperial prerogative, so the Emperor must have granted a special privilege to Liu Sheng and his wife. In pre-Han burials, jade pieces were often placed in the body's orifices, because this stone, especially valued by the Chinese since Lungshan neolithic times, was credited with powers of preserving the corpse. The climax of this expectation was the total encasement offered by the Han suits— an extravagance abandoned soon afterwards. Liu Sheng's spirit must be reflecting ruefully upon the few shrivelled teeth which were the sole remnants of him to be found within the suit.

Liu Sheng has decayed, but the skills of his nameless craftsmen endure. This gave no slight satisfaction to his Communist discoverers, who knew that this prince, described by Ssu-ma Ch'ien as a lover of women and drink, had been given such a lavish funeral at a time when thousands of his subjects were dying of starvation caused by disastrous floods. His jade craftsmen, who must have worked for more than a year, had cut out over 2,000 pieces of jade, each about one eighth of an inch (0.35 cm) thick and mostly square, but many with irregular shapes carefully designed to fit the body's curves. The cutting of jade, which is harder than any metal, is done with abrasive powder rather than with a saw edge, and is a very lengthy operation. Tiny holes were then drilled at each corner of every piece, which were then sewn together with twelve-stranded gold thread tied in nine beautifully varied knots. The pieces were first assembled in ten separated sections, such as head, face, arms and gloves, each edged with red cloth which in some sections was piped with iron wire. The front and back chest sections of Tou Wan's suit were, exceptionally, joined with silk thread. When the prince and princess, for whom these suits must have been carefully measured, finally breathed their expected last, the ten pieces were sewn around them in a tightly fitting, totally enveloping suit. Then the corpse was laid in a coffin, its head resting on a bronze pillow inlaid with gold and filled with wild pepper. Liu Sheng's hands were laid across his belly, grasping ceremonial jade crescents; an iron knife was placed by his left side and two iron swords by his right.

The recovery of these two suits was an immensely intricate operation. Although nothing in the tombs had been disturbed, perishable materials such as wood and bone had not survived. The jade suits had collapsed and the gold thread had frayed and snapped. Tou Wan's coffin had been cased in slabs of jade and as the coffin decayed these had fallen in on the suit. The excavators found her eternal rest reduced to a dust-compacted jumble of jade. Before they could concentrate on the suit itself, this mass had to be cleared by scraping with a small knife, prising with a bamboo spatula and cleaning each stage with a fine brush, taking infinite care not to displace any of the underlying pieces.

The actual reconstruction of the suit was a task for the laboratory and thither all the pieces had to go, without destroying any evidence about the original position of each piece. Where any number of pieces still held together, the excavators first bounded the section with stiff wire and then threaded more flexible wires underneath, strand by strand, until a basket had been formed. Over this were laid several layers of soft paper and the whole was then set in plaster of Paris, to be finally lifted off in a block. Where the jade pieces were loose and scattered, each piece was photographed, drawn and numbered before being individually moved. When safely deposited in the laboratory, each piece had to be cleaned with extreme care so

Central chamber of the cave-tomb of Liu Sheng.

that no traces of the original thread were destroyed and the laborious work of reassembly was begun.

Liu Sheng was reduced to a few teeth. But the Marquess of Tai, who had died half a century earlier, made a far more dramatic re-entry into this world in 1971, when archaeologists uncovered her in almost exactly the same state as she had been in when buried. She

Excavating the hill-top grave pit at Ma-wang-tui.

OPPOSITE
View down into the pit of the Marquess of Tai's grave, with the lids of the coffins removed and showing the grave-goods stacked in the four side-chambers. Ma-wang-tui, Hunan province, c. 150 BC.

was found, when a hospital was being built at Ma-wang-tui near Ch'ang-sha railway station in Hunan, in one of the well-known 'fire-pit' graves of that region. They are so-named because, when first broken open, a wave of highly inflammable marsh gas rushes out, which has occasionally incinerated the nocturnal robber unwise enough to carry a torch or lamp with an open flame.

The very large number of graves around Ch'ang-sha was mentioned in the previous chapter; the flourishing civilisation of Ch'u endured as a major cultural centre of the empire. The graves are renowned for two contrasting conditions: either the contents are found in a state of extreme decay, often with no sign of corpse or coffin, or, rarely, they are extraordinarily well preserved. The decay is caused by the heavy rainfall and water-sodden ground of the rice-growing region of the Yangtze basin. The remarkable exceptions are probably due to the fact that, when a grave is constructed tightly enough to keep out all this damp, it must also be impregnable to every other destructive intrusion. Marsh gas is produced by a bacteria which can only grow when all oxygen is excluded, and this may be a reason

for its presence in these exceptional graves. The Ma-wang-tui grave was lined with a very dense white clay, and damp-absorbing charcoal was packed between this and a six-walled wooden coffin structure; the whole presenting an extremely efficient insulation. Inside lay the white-skinned Marquess of Tai, hands resting on her portly stomach and mouth wide open to hold a ceremonial jade, dressed in twenty silken cloaks and wraps, tied in a neat bundle with nine bands of silk and covered by two beautifully decorated quilts. After being disinterred she was carried off to the local hospital for preservative treatment and X-rays. Her arm, when injected, swelled in reaction and then slowly relaxed again. A later autopsy revealed that she had died of heart failure due to 'biliary colic' and that her last hours were spent eating 138 melon pips.

Chinese history has many stories, from as long ago as fifteen hundred years, of ancient corpses discovered 'as though living'. The Marquess of Tai has given modern scholars the first scientifically observed evidence that such tales can no longer be dismissed as nonsense and she has become the subject of intense excitement and speculation. A plate of strawberry plums found in the tomb chamber indicated that the funeral must have taken place in May, during the short season this fruit enjoys. But someone dying at this time would almost certainly have carried with them to the grave the eggs of the small flies that, to judge from the evidence of many other graves, commonly hatched in the coffin and fed on the corpse. There was no sign of such insect life in the Marquess' coffin and so it is suggested that she died in the cold of winter, lying encoffined for several months before the funeral rites were completed. Whether or not any oils or other preparations were used deliberately to preserve the corpse is still the subject of research, but it is quite possible, since such preservation was much desired by a superstitious belief in the spirit life, and was also encouraged by the obligations of filial piety, a crux of Confucian ethics.

These attitudes towards life and death led to lavish burials for which the early Han was famous. We still have records of a great debate raised in 81 BC by stern critics of the degenerate 'modern' ways. The Marquess' husband was prime minister to the Prince of Ch'ang-sha and the wealth accruing from such a post in this flourishing district is reflected in the lavishness of her funeral. But the ostentation condemned by the critics has become the archaeologists' windfall. Although the Marquess did not have a jade suit to mark her rank, this rank was shown by the four elaborately painted coffins

OPPOSITE
Above Flying horse poised on a swallow from Wu-wei in Kansu, Western Han dynasty.
Below Gilt bronze lamp, inscribed 'Lamp of the Palace of Eternal Trust', from the tomb of Tou Wan.

Musicians with mouth-organs and citherns, from the grave retinue of the Marquess of Tai.

contained one within another, by the number of her shrouds and by the luxurious supplies that accompanied her into the afterworld. The entire contents of her tomb had been inventoried on 312 slips of bamboo. These bamboo slips, which were originally tied together side by side in a sequence for rolling up, were the usual format for written records until they were replaced by silk and then paper in the Later Han period.

The lavish burial, preserved by so uncommon a fate, revealed to the archaeologists such a variety of surprises that it is difficult to make a selection. The food supplies buried with the Marquess had become somewhat dessicated but easy to recognise, with plates of chicken drumsticks, fish and spareribs laid out on trays, and young chickens, eggs and bean flour packed in picnic boxes. The lacquer objects, such as jars, cups, bowls and chopsticks, are astounding in their lustrous freshness. Han lacquer work is famed, but the vast majority of surviving examples are crinkled and warped by shrinkage of the wooden body. Stuffed among the dishes and boxes were 162 wooden figurines of servants, musicians and other members of the household. They vary in height from one to three feet, some are painted and others are clothed. The number may well be an accurate reflection of the size of the Marquess' domestic establishment.

Above Portrait of a lady and her attendants, probably the Marquess of Tai, occupant of the tomb at Ma-wang-tui, Hunan. A detail from the painted banner shown on page 100. *Below* Lacquer cups from the tomb at Ma-wang-tui.

The fame of this tomb may eventually rest mainly on its treasury of silk and clothes. No complete specimen of Han clothing had been found before. The dressing of the corpse has already been mentioned,

97

and this was supplemented by a great variety of other wear and personal effects, such as coats, gloves, socks, false hair and combs, neatly packed in sets of lacquer boxes. In the western side-chamber of the tomb were tightly stacked over forty fine basket-weave boxes and these contained over fifty rolls of silk; enough spare material to keep generations of ghostly sempstresses at work. This wealth of fabrics reduces all earlier finds almost to insignificance. It included silk and hemp in a great variety of weaves, from 'floating mist' gauze (sixty-two warp threads per cm.) to dense silk (up to two hundred warp threads per cm.). Some are single-coloured, others multi-coloured; some are printed and others are embroidered. They provide an unmatched dictionary of early Han decorative motifs.

The single most remarkable silk item was a painted T-shaped banner, which had been laid over the coffin. It had the remains of a bamboo frame, showing that it had probably been held aloft in front of the hearse, or 'spirit carriage' as the Chinese call it, leading on the spirit in its procession to the grave. To express this purpose the entire banner is covered with superbly drawn and richly coloured pictures, which witness to the art of a highly sophisticated painter. The centre panel depicts a somewhat bowed, elderly woman leaning on a staff; three ladies stand in attendance behind and two kneeling servants offer up trays of food before her. This must be the Marquess herself. Medical examination of the corpse showed her to be in her fifties, with a deformed back, and the excavators claim that the face is a recognisable likeness. The platform on which these figures are placed is held by dragons elegantly twining in the form of a stand for a musical stone, a principal instrument in courtly music. The crescentic stone hangs from the centre of the stand, poised like a roof over two rows of servants flanking a sacrificial offering of food.

The interpretation of the entire pictorial scheme is a matter of lively debate among Chinese scholars. But all agree that the 'under-world' is represented at the bottom and the 'heavens' at the top, with earth somewhere in between. The most convincing explanation is that it shows the deceased's acceptance into the spirit world, the gates of which open above her. But we must remember that the Chinese did not conceive of a 'heaven above' in the Christian manner.

All the levels on the banner are peopled with a fascinating variety of mythological creatures. Some of these are well known, such as the lady Ch'ang-ngo who fled to the moon and lived there as an immortal toad. She appears here in both forms beside the moon in the upper left corner. Opposite is the sun in the upper right, within the sun is its

The wrapped corpse of the Marquess of Tai.

personification, the raven, and below it other suns rest in the branches of a mulberry tree. The myth of multiple suns is one of exceptionally wide interest, occurring in many countries throughout the world. Several creatures in the banner scenes have not been identified.

It is worth remembering that Ch'ang-sha is in the heartland of the Ch'u culture, renowned in the Han period for the richness and distinctiveness of its superstitions. The *Songs of Ch'u*, written during that and earlier periods, are a mine of mythology and contain many images similar to those on the banner, such as:

'O soul come back! Climb not up to the heaven above.
For tigers and leopards guard the gates, with jaws every ready to rend mortal men . . .
O soul, come back! Go not down to the Land of Darkness,
Where the Earth God lies, nine-coiled, with dreadful horns on his forehead,
And a great humped back and bloody thumbs, pursuing men, swift-footed . . .'

The Marquess of Tai unwrapped.

The silk which so richly furnished the Marquess' grave was a distinctive Chinese product and had been so since Shang times at the latest. By the Han period its fame had spread as far as Rome, where China was known as the Land of Silk. The camel trains laden with silk-bales that left the Han capital trekked out along the Kansu corridor, through Wu-wei and Tun-huang and onwards north and south of the Tarim Desert basin, through Samarkand and on to Antioch; a route that has become famous under the name of 'the Silk Road'. The Emperor Wu-ti waged vigorous war against resurgent Hsiung-nu tribes threatening these northern areas, and the protection of vital commercial routes was one of his major concerns. Chinese garrisons guarded far-flung frontier posts and their remains have sometimes been revealed to the present age by drifting desert sands; the first discoveries of Han silks came from these sites.

In October 1969 a general's tomb of the second century AD, discovered near Wu-wei, yielded a very different treasure. In the front chambers of this brick-built tomb were found many bronze statuettes, including thirty-nine horses, fourteen carts and twenty-eight human figures. This find astonished the archaeologists, because they had already realised from its entrance that the tomb had twice been robbed. The statuettes, many of which have inscriptions such as 'Slave of Mr Chang', are now counted among the finest known works of Han art. Few works have so rapidly won their fame as has the

Painted silk funeral
banner, placed on the
coffin of the Marquess
of Tai. *See plate facing
page 97 for colour detail.*

'Flying Horse', its head and tail raised high in a proudly untrammelled gallop, its fleeting touch with the earth brilliantly suggested in the one hoof borne on a flying swallow. These horses were originally brightly painted; the bared teeth were white, the flaring lips red, the eyes white, red and black. Of the sculptor we know nothing at all; but neither the presence nor the quality of the horses need surprise us, for horses had become an obsession with Han rulers.

The reasons for this went back to the adoption of cavalry by Chinese armies around 300 BC, mentioned in the last chapter. The campaigns against the Hsiung-nu demanded vast numbers of war horses with qualities of size, stamina and muscle not possessed by indigenous breeds. The Hsiung-nu rode a breed derived from the wild 'Przhevalski' horse of Siberia, a sturdy but rather short animal some thirteen hands high and no bigger than a pony. The constant struggle of the Chinese to acquire adequate stocks of such mounts entailed many furious battles with the Hsiung-nu. Nomads were sometimes ready to offer horses in trade for Chinese silk, but Wu-ti heard that two thousand miles away in Ferghana, the region of modern Afghanistan, great steeds of sixteen hands were bred. In pursuit of such marvels he embarked on military campaigns of fanatic, even lunatic ambition, which culminated in an army of sixty thousand men and thirty thousand horses marching out towards Ferghana in 102 BC. They reached the capital city of that country, successfully besieged it and returned to China with a great haul of the famous Ferghana steeds, although at a cost of five-sixths of their original force. The town of Wu-wei, a staging-post on the route to Central Asia, must have seen the returning remnants of this fantastic expedition. Over the ensuing years it must also have seen many fine horses, both of the nomads' breed and of the famed 'Heavenly Horses' from Ferghana, which were sometimes brought through as tribute and were now bred within China. The general was perhaps an equine connoisseur, taking with him to the grave the finest Han portrayal of a horse known to us. Its high and arching neck, long-striding legs and proud eyes in a noble forehead mark it as being of the Heavenly breed. Such a horse was admired by the eighth-century poet Tu Fu:

'The Ferghana horse is famed among nomad breeds.
Lean in build, like the point of a lance;
Two ears sharp as bamboo spikes;
Four hoofs light as though born of the wind.
Heading away across the endless spaces,
Truly, you may entrust him with your life . . .'

9

Buddhism and the Chinese Tradition

The Han court during the second century AD suffered under increasingly intense struggles between the clans of empresses and the adopted families of palace eunuchs, while government control slipped away into the hands of aristocratic families consolidating themselves in the provinces. This disintegration of an empire, finally overwhelmed by its own institutional and economic complexities, has often been compared with the contemporary decline of the Roman Empire. Among the many points of comparison is the germination of a religion that in due time, like Christianity in the Western empire, was to achieve immense influence. Buddhism, of course, was new only on Chinese soil, for the Buddha himself had died in 483 BC in north-east India. Probably during the lifetime of Christ, his faith was transplanted to China where, from a quiet beginning, it grew steadily as the climate of society became more favourable. Confucianism ordered man and his behaviour in relation to the imperial state. The ultimate aim of Buddhism was release from the worldly state; it formed a much broader image of man and opened great psychological and spiritual vistas. As the Confucian state crumbled, intellectuals pondered fresh answers and a rebellious proletariat sought for a light in their misery. Buddhism appeared to many as a saving grace.

The Han dynasty finally broke up into the Three Kingdoms, ruled by three generals who had orchestrated the dynastic death throes. The ensuing period of violent conflict was one which benefited none but Buddhism and nomad tribes along China's northern marches. These latter gained an increasing foothold in the north, forcing a southwards migration of such families as had sufficient wealth and independence to make the move. This was a major factor in shaping the next five centuries which, throughout a constant struggle for power between a succession of leading families, remained roughly divided between non-Chinese control of the north and Chinese control of the south.

The most famous southern dynasty was the Eastern Chin (317–420), which established its capital at the city in Kiangsu province nowadays called Nanking ('Southern Capital'). Ever since this moment Kiangsu has remained a leading centre of China's civilisation. The main intellectual developments in Chinese Buddhism were the achievement of Eastern Chin scholars. They debated endlessly over the relationship between Buddhism and the native Taoism (pronounced Dow-ism), a philosophy going back to Chuang Chou, one of the great Eastern Chou thinkers. For the Chinese, Taoism has long been paired with Confucianism as the other side of the human coin; its speculative, intuitive and deeply poetic thought providing a perfect complement. Although Taoism had accreted many mystical practices and folk superstitions, it was in no sense a religion. It offered escape to individuals but no salvation to society and so initially was no competitor for Buddhism. On the contrary, for Chinese seeking to fit Buddhist thought into their own intellectual world, Taoism provided many fascinating parallels.

Many of the men debating these problems withdrew from official life as Confucian ideals went into a temporary eclipse, and turned instead to contemplation of nature and cultivation of the fine arts. The Eastern Chin marks the first, and one of the finest, flowerings of China's classic three artistic diversions: poetry, calligraphy and painting. Calligraphy, the art of writing with a fine, pointed brush, is for the Chinese the noblest form of visual art. Its history is interwoven with their traditional archaeology, the study of inscriptions on stone. Modern archaeological discoveries have provoked some very lively arguments about the classic styles of Eastern Chin calligraphers but, up to date, it has made a much more dramatic impact on our knowledge of Eastern Chin pictorial art. Painting is a sister-art of calligraphy, albeit a junior, because the Chinese painter and calligrapher use the same brush and in a similar manner. All the Eastern Chin originals on silk and paper have long since perished, but archaeology has partially repaired this almost total gap in our knowledge by the discovery of pictorial decorations in tombs. One of the finest examples is a series of impressed bricks which lined a tomb found in 1960 at Hsi-shan-ch'iao in Nanking. This illustration of a row of gentlemen sitting under trees must have originally been executed with the traditional Chinese brush, wielded by an artist of superbly fluent elegance. They are particularly interesting because he has added their names, showing them to be portraits of the 'Seven Sages of the Bamboo Grove', who had lived near Loyang in the third century and formed the most famous literary coterie in Chinese history. We see them at their cultured leisure: men such as Hsi K'ang, China's supreme lutenist; the poet Juan Chi, who would 'climb mountains to gaze down on waters, forgetting to return for days on end'; and the Taoist Shan T'ao, who later disgusted his friends by accepting a high official post. These were men at the roots of the Southern Tradition in Chinese culture, and the artist, who quite possibly took their portraits from a famous composition, represents the artistic side of that tradition.

After the fall of the Han, the north-west remained for a long time a haven of comparative peace, isolated from the great upheavals further east. Since the traffic with Central Asia passed through this region, along the Kansu corridor, it continued largely uninterrupted. At the extreme north-west of Chinese territory lay the oasis town of Tun-huang, a gateway at the junction of the routes running north and south of the Tarim Desert basin. In the third century, efficient irrigation and agricultural techniques brought to this town a comfort and a prosperity which must have gladdened the eyes of many a dust-caked traveller and wearied merchant. It was through the lands that these men traversed far to the west, by Kashgar and across the Pamirs, that the faith of the Buddha had spread to China, as monasteries grew up in the oasis towns which have since faded into the sands. By the first century AD, Buddhist communities had followed the traders into the cities of Ch'ang-an and Loyang, and many of the

The three Taoists, Hsi K'ang, Juan Chi and Shan T'ao. Designs impressed on bricks in a tomb at Hsi-shan-ch'iao, Nanking.

earliest Buddhist travellers must have passed through Tun-huang.

For the faithful so far from the cradle of their faith, one of the most pressing needs was for the holy scriptures. The texts of Buddhism are peculiarly extensive and in that age were increasing steadily. Even after a copy of a new *sūtra* had been reverently carried through the great trek from India, it was still in a language understood by extremely few of the Chinese congregation. For this reason, many of the outstanding milestones in the first centuries of Chinese Buddhism are the works of famed translators. Tun-huang was a centre for such scholarly enterprises, supported by its thriving monasteries.

In the year 366 a monk at Tun-huang had a vision of a thousand Buddhas ascending over the low hills which lie twelve miles south-east of the town. Out of this came an ambition, modelled on a practice which had spread from India, to honour these Buddhas by carving out cave-shrines in the hills. So began a great work, which is today one of China's wonders. Stretching for a mile along the sandstone cliffs is a honeycomb of caves, their closely packed mouths opening side by side and on several levels, sometimes as many as four. 486 of these caves contain groups of clay statues which, together with every inch of the walls, are painted in a glorious riot of colour. It is for this painting that Tun-huang is nowadays so famous. Its subjects range from individual cult figures, through narratives of the Buddha's life, to lavish scenes of paradise, filled with vignettes from everyday life and framed by richly varied decorative motifs. The paintings and statues were created mainly during the fifth to the eleventh centuries, with some additions down to the fourteenth century; and over the first century they show a clear change from a western to a purely Chinese style. Before recent discoveries of early tomb paintings, these vigorous works by anonymous artists far from the centre of China's civilisation were almost our only examples of actual painting in China before the ninth century. In sheer quantity they will never be matched.

The Thousand Buddha Caves are an historical monument of uncommon size, but as an historical monument they are a rediscovery. They survived material decay, largely thanks to the extremely dry climate. They survived human assault, largely because Tun-huang's fortunes were linked with Central Asia, rather than with Central China. In 845, for example, a ferocious persecution of Buddhism almost completely destroyed China's Buddhist heritage of eight centuries, but at this time Tun-huang was under Tibetan occupation. After the great persecution, Buddhism in China declined into a

A musician. Figure on a tomb tile with moulded design, Teng-hsien in Honan province, fifth century.

Mourners at the
physical death of the
Buddha; a wall-
painting in the Tun-
huang caves showing
western influences on
subject and style.
Painted during the
early ninth-century
Tibetan occupation of
Tun-huang.

minor cultural role, but the community at Tun-huang hung together,
often under alien rule, until the fourteenth century, when China
completely turned her back on Central Asia in favour of expanding
sea routes to the south. Tun-huang died. A small resettlement
programme under the Manchu Ch'ing dynasty restored a degree of
life and the caves were re-occupied by a few monks, but they remained
otherwise unknown.

In the late nineteenth and early twentieth century, Central Asia
became a magnet for foreign explorers, who were drawn to its vast
desert tracts in a search for remains of a Buddhist civilisation which
reportedly had once flourished there. Count Szechenyi from
Hungary, Count Otani from Japan, Professor Chavannes from
France, Colonel Kozloff from Russia; their scientific curiosity and
their treasure hunting, their specialised knowledge and far-ranging
vision, their genuine humility and unshakable conviction of superi-
ority, all run typically as the weft and warp of the fabric of that
extraordinary age. One of the most remarkable was an Englishman,

Sir Aurel Stein, who trekked through Central Asia on three separate occasions under the aegis of the Indian Government's Archaeological Survey. Between 1901 and 1916 he covered 25,000 miles on horseback and his own feet, accompanied by servants such as Chiang Ssu-yeh, his 'devoted Chinese comrade, ever ready to face hardships for the sake of my scientific interests'; his 'handyman, brave Naik Ram Singh'; his 'feckless Kashmiri cook'; and, 'nearest to my heart', his fox-terrier Dash.

In March 1907, after trudging for three weeks across salt-bed and gravel without seeing another living soul, Stein's caravan stepped with relief into the sudden greenness of Tun-huang. Stein had heard of the Thousand Buddha Caves, which were one of his destinations. They far surpassed his expectations and, in addition, he soon heard rumours of a quite unexpected treasure. This was said to be a hoard of ancient documents found in a walled-up niche. Although no one had much idea of what they were, the Governor of Kansu had apparently ordered them to be kept locked in the niche under the guard of a humble monk, who had taken upon himself the care of the caves. Stein and his assistant Chiang, with very great difficulty, persuaded the suspicious guardian to open up the niche for their inspection. In Stein's words, 'There appeared a solid mass of manuscript bundles rising to ten feet from the floor and filling, as subsequent measurement showed, close on 500 cubic feet.' The unfortunate monk found, willy-nilly, his two persecutors permanently established in the cave while he himself hauled out the bundles, pile after pile and day after day, as Stein glanced through them in growing amazement. The cache, which later research revealed had been walled up in 1035 when the region was threatened by an invasion, was so well preserved that almost the only damage suffered was through the sheer weight of material. Stein found that the manuscripts, dating from the fifth century onwards, embraced an extraordinary range of languages; Chinese and Tibetan, Sanskrit from India, Sogdian, Khotanese, Kuchean and other lost tongues of Central Asia. There were also painted and embroidered banners, their colours faded not at all over the centuries. Such a store was obviously nothing less than the library of the monastic community.

Through a most devious campaign, with promises of rich recompense, Stein and Chiang prised from the monk's guardianship various miscellaneous bundles. But Stein was determined to gain some of the most jealously valued items, the ancient Chinese *sūtras*. After many weeks of persuasion, the monk agreed to sell. On that occasion

Cave temples of the
Thousand Buddhas at
Tun-huang.
The wooden facade
of the original complex
had disappeared by
the time Sir Aurel
Stein took this photo-
graph.

Stein had stealthily to summon others in his party to make a midnight
trip, carrying sacks of manuscripts under the trees along the river and
back to his tent.

Stein was eventually forced to flee by official pressure and a
brewing local revolt against the Manchu government, but his haul
had been crated and was on its way to the British Museum, where the
twenty-nine cases arrived sixteen months later. Other manuscripts

from the cache were acquired by later visitors, especially the great French sinologue Paul Pelliot, who also made a major survey of the entire cave complex. Ultimately only a minority remained in China, a fact about which the Chinese are more than regretful. The caves finally came under the protection of the National Tun-huang Institute in 1943 and today there is a continuous programme of maintenance and research.

Cave shrines spread through North China in the fifth century, a spread which was greatly assisted by the support given to Buddhism by rulers of the non-Chinese states. Buddhism, being wholly independent of Confucian concepts of legitimate authority, was an ideal religion for espousal by rulers who were illegitimate by Chinese lights. It found its greatest patrons in emperors of the Turkic Wei dynasty who, from the founding of their dynasty in 386 until its collapse in 534, successfully pursued a consolidation of North China which did much to prepare for the Sui re-unification of 589. Their capital was at Ta-t'ung, just south of the Great Wall, and in the 460s an enormous project of cave temples was begun at Yun-kang, a few miles west of this capital. The giant figures of Buddhas, rising to a height of seventy feet, were to honour the past emperors and were worshipped as such. There was no painting of murals here, but the cave walls were exuberantly covered with narrative and decorative carving. Originally the cliffs were faced with elaborate wooden temples and the whole area was a flourishing religious retreat. When Professor Chavannes discovered the site in 1907 it was an abandoned wilderness. Later it was cleared and extensively surveyed by Japanese scholars in one of the many excellent archaeological enterprises which were a strange accompaniment to the otherwise vicious Japanese occupation of Chinese territory from 1937 to 1945.

In 494, while the caves at Yun-kang were still under construction, the Wei emperor abandoned the flourishing and populous centre which had so laboriously been established at Ta-t'ung, and moved his capital to Loyang. This was a profoundly significant event, a symbolic step into the heartland of Chinese civilisation and a statement of that extraordinary transformation which overtook almost every outsider to rule on Chinese soil. Near the new capital, the laborious carving of imperial cave temples began afresh, at Lung-men, seven miles south of the city. The relationship between Yun-kang and Lung-men is of great interest to the art historian, for it shows the same emergence of purely Chinese forms out of Indian and Central Asian models as is seen at Tun-huang. Late Wei sculpture

Bronze figure of the Buddha, Wei dynasty, first half of the sixth century.

achieves an ethereal reality which raises it to a position of greatness in the world's religious art.

In 515 the Wei throne passed to an heir aged only six years and, as a result, power fell into the hands of the Empress Dowager Ling. She was an ardent Buddhist who brought the fortunes of her faith to a dazzling pinnacle, but, of all her vast expense of money and effort on religious structures, the only material evidence to survive is the caves constructed at Lung-men during her rule. The caves enjoyed a second period of glory at the end of the seventh century, when Buddhism reached its final apogee under a lady of striking similarity to the Dowager Empress Ling, the Empress Wu, who declared herself to be a Buddha incarnate.

Buddhism and the indigenous Chinese tradition were like the tides of two seas rising to an extraordinary height and overflowing into each other across a dividing continent. But little is known of the inroads made by Chinese culture across Central Asia and far beyond Tun-huang. Between 1966 and 1969 a large cemetery was excavated near Turfan in the far north of Sinkiang. This, the Uighur Autonomous Region of today, is where the northern desert route once passed, arching over the lifeless Tarim basin. The graves date from the third to the eighth centuries and contained interesting evidence of a

The Lung-men caves: the great Buddha at Feng-hsien-ssu, carved at the orders of the Empress Wu *c*. 700 AD.

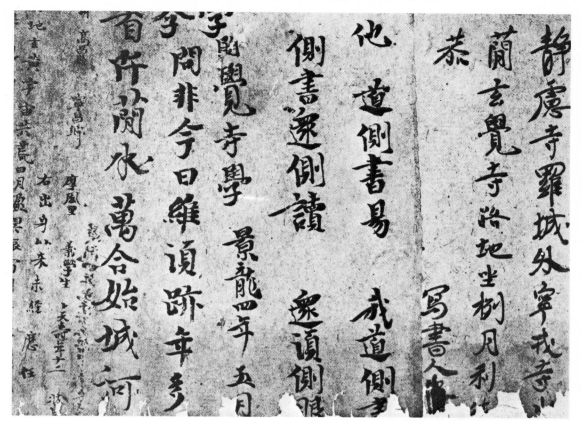

Section of a scroll text of *The Analects of Confucius*, with a note at the end, 'Student at the local school, Pu T'ien-shou, aged ten'. It is dated 710 AD.

growing Chinese influence. The most remarkable piece actually dates from 710, well into the T'ang dynasty, but it reflects a situation going back to pre-T'ang times. It is a paper scroll, over fifteen feet (5·38 metres) long, on which a young boy has practised writing out *The Analects of Confucius*, signing himself 'Student at the local school, Pu T'ien-shou, aged ten'. Although incomplete and with a number of childish errors, it is the earliest known manuscript copy of this 'bible' of China's civilisation. There is another manuscript that was found in the foundations of a house in the same region and which dates from the early ninth century. It is a few doggerel verses, composed and written down by a member of an Uighur family that had apparently been struggling for three generations to acquire a Chinese education. One verse reads:

'Tired of study the young lad soon does grow,
That there's money in books he does not know.
How much is there?—If only I'd known,
I'd have turned up my lamp and studied till dawn!'

10

The Imperial Tombs of the T'ang

The historian Ssu-ma Ch'ien, writing around 100 BC, declared that, 'The Way of the Three Dynasties [of Hsia, Shang and Chou] is like a cycle that, when it ends, must begin again.' Such a reassuring view of history can hardly be accepted by the modern historian, but, had he been alive, Ssu-ma Ch'ien would have been a gratified observer of events around the opening of the seventh century AD.

The political confusion rampant during the four centuries following the collapse of the Han was cleared away by a man who seemed a re-incarnation of Ch'in-Shih-huang. He declared himself first emperor of the Sui dynasty in 589, with its capital in Ch'ang-an, and supported his military unification of the country with measures such as the reconstruction of the Great Wall and the expansion of canals into a great system connecting all China's major waterways. Yet after only twenty-eight years the ambition of the second ruler of the Sui empire over-reached itself and fell before rebels under the leadership of the Li clan. In 618 Li Yuan, once a general at the Sui court, established himself in the Ch'ang-an palace and declared himself first emperor of the T'ang, a dynasty which was destined to match the glory of the Han and whose civilisation was unrivalled in the world of that age. The second emperor, T'ang T'ai-tsung, is justly acknowledged as one of the greatest rulers the world has known. His conquests extended Chinese suzerainty westwards to the upper Indus valley, southwards into North Vietnam, and those of his successor went eastwards through the Korean peninsula. T'ai-tsung was one of his country's leading intellects and artists, his government was enormously wealthy, highly centralised, very efficient and for the time comparatively humane.

OPPOSITE
Above Wall-painting of attendants in the tomb of Princess Yung-t'ai. *Below* Tomb figurines from a tomb near Loyang, T'ang dynasty.

OPPOSITE
The Spirit Road to the
tomb mound of the
Empress Wu.

The T'ang emperors were the last to follow the ancient tradition of establishing a capital at Ch'ang-an, the 'City of Eternal Peace', but simultaneously they set up a second Eastern Capital at Loyang in Honan. They often moved between the two, governed by such considerations of pleasure and practicality as climate and the supply of food. The Eastern Capital became increasingly popular, and the T'ang dynasty marked a final eastwards shift of China's cultural, agricultural and political centre. However, at the height of T'ang power Ch'ang-an was the greatest city on earth, with a million people living within its gates. The walls encompassed a rectangle more than six miles long, divided into a grid of absolute symmetry by streets running from north to south and from east to west. The imperial palaces and government offices occupied a ninth of this area, in the centre of its north side, and a great highway five hundred feet wide, ran straight from the palaces down to the main South Gate.

The plan of this tremendous metropolis, which must have astounded thousands of foreign visitors every year, has been transmitted through descriptions of contemporaries and an eleventh-century map, and archaeologists have been able to confirm it by a number of fragmentary excavations. But most Chinese buildings supported their roofs by wooden pillars and beams, while walls had no structural function and were often quite insubstantial, leaving few traces for the archaeologist. The ideal of permanence in this world, which supported so many great buildings elsewhere and which has left us with so many important remains, was not a customary concern of the Chinese.

The modern city on the site of Ch'ang-an is Sian, and when it was visited in 1923 by Langdon Warner, one of the prescient scholars responsible for the great collections of Chinese art acquired by American museums around that time, he found it a city of fascinating but somewhat shabby appearance, covering an area no larger than the original enclosure of imperial palaces and government offices. But in the city Warner saw four huge stone slabs, each carved with a magnificent image of a horse. These slabs, which were then leaning sadly against the courtyard walls of a small museum, belonged to a set of six which had been dragged from the mausoleum of the Emperor T'ai-tsung. As Warner later wrote, these 'were happily safe from our American dollars. The other two, somewhat split and battered, are the pride of the University Museum in Philadelphia.'

The superb power of these horses reminds us at once of the Han bronze horses from Wu-wei and reflects an even higher value placed

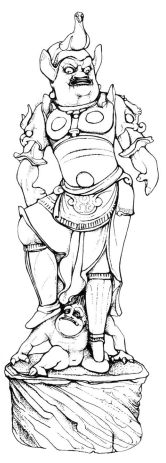

Pottery tomb guardian, eighth century.

113

on cavalry by the military might of the T'ang, which strained China's silk industry by an annual requirement of fifty million feet of silk for the purchase of horses from Turkic tribes. The six steeds of T'ai-tsung are the most renowned horses in China's history, for they bore him through his military triumphs, were eulogised by the Emperor himself and were painted by the most famous artist of the day. In 636 their portraits were cut in stone and these monuments were eventually set up at his mausoleum after his death in 649.

Horses were a measure of wealth and power: 'born of the dragon race', their nobility and strength became enduring images in China's poetry and painting. In T'ang tombs horse figurines are of unusual quality and quantity, and this is related to social status; an edict of 667, for example, forbade the riding of horses by traders and artisans. The figurine illustrated on the jacket of this book is a superb example of both this status and the martial qualities so admired by the imperial riders, for it was found in a royal tomb, that of Crown Prince I-te. The three-tufted mane shows royal rank and it was one of a pair that faced each other inside the tomb's stone portals, the leaders of several hundred pottery horses on parade in the side-chambers. The father of this prince was the Emperor Chung-tsung (died 710), who was no warrior such as his grandfather T'ai-tsung had been and whose horses were famed for deeds more effete than those of the Six Chargers. Their talent was for dancing, and we have a description of a performance they put on for a visiting Tibetan mission:

'... They were all fitted and comparisoned with silk thread, pigmented in five colours, with garnishings of gold ... When the music was played, each of the horses followed it, fluently responsive, and when they came to the middlemost stanza, the performers of the music gave them wine to drink, at which they took up the cups in their mouths; then they lay down, and got up again. The Tibetans were greatly astonished.'

We would hardly expect archaeology to support this description of one wonder among a legion, but in fact it did so gracefully in 1970, by the discovery in Sian of a silver saddle-bottle, bearing a golden image of one of the Emperor's bibulous horses. We will return at the end of this chapter to the peculiar significance of this find.

Chung-tsung's son, the Crown Prince I-te, had a remarkable and miserable fate, his short life falling within one of China's most extraordinary eras, the reign of the Empress Wu. The popular account of this lady has no doubts in its judgement. She first achieved

Camel with foreign musicians, perhaps Persian. Tomb figurine of the eighth century.

Silver saddle-bottle with a gold figure of a dancing horse, from the Prince of Pin's treasure at Sian, *c*.700 AD.

eminence as a favoured concubine of T'ai-tsung, retired into a nunnery upon his death, re-emerged and then through a process of dastardly intrigue and unscrupulous cruelty, became the Empress of his succeeding son, whom she dominated utterly. Within a short while of his death, she had pushed his successor, the Emperor Chung-tsung, out of sight and declared herself Empress of a new Chou dynasty. She manœuvred her own family, the Wu clan, into power and waged a campaign of terror against the Li clan of her former husband, causing hundreds of them to be put to death. On her death-bed she was forced into abdication and in 705 a somewhat enfeebled Chung-tsung was resuscitated, restoring the Great T'ang. As a villainess her reputation is probably unmatched, obscuring the fact that she was a ruler of genius. It was she, fighting against the stranglehold of the old aristocratic families, who opened the government to the highly educated gentry and brought about a fundamental revolution in the social, intellectual and political history of China. It was she who most clearly realised that China's centre of gravity had shifted eastwards. She was also an ardent Buddhist, finding in that religion a justification for female rule which was totally denied her by Confucianism, and she patronised the last phase of Buddhist sculpture in the Lung-men caves outside the Eastern Capital.

Crown Prince I-te was the posthumous title of Li Ch'ung-jun, a youthfully rash opponent of the Empress. In 701 he was overheard to criticise two brothers who had wormed their way into court as her favourites, and he paid for this with his life. His tomb is one of a group of three which have been excavated in recent years with the aim of elucidating this crucial struggle between the Li and Wu clans. The two other tombs belong to Li Ch'ung-jun's sister, Li Hsien-hui, and to their uncle, Li Hsien. The sister's tomb was excavated between 1960 and 1962, the other two between 1970 and 1972.

Hsien-hui was the Emperor Chung-tsung's sixth daughter and in 700, at the age of sixteen, left the confines of the Inner Palace to marry a grand-nephew of the Empress Wu. But the enmity between the two families was too great to be assuaged even by the royal custom of marriage between cousins. Hsien-hui's husband joined his brother-in-law in criticising the Empress's favourites and with him suffered the fatal consequences. The popular account is that Hsien-hui was also implicated and that all three were either ordered to commit suicide, or were beaten to death. However, in the past, historians have been faced with conflicting accounts, and now the excavation of the sister's tomb has provided a different answer.

In the tomb was found her memorial, a stone table about three and a half feet square, its sides delicately carved with enchantingly dancing forms of flowers and animals and its top carved with a long inscription. The phraseology is typical of the highly stylised forms of Chinese ceremonial prose and is virtually unintelligible to anyone not steeped in millennia of Chinese learning. After hymning the ecstacies of her marriage, it continues: 'After the coiled dragon suffered under the sharp and martial sword, the hen phoenix grieved with her solitary shadow. But before the fire on the cedar tree had departed, the boat of cypress was drifting empty and the full-moon pearl was shattered. Bitter that there was no fragrance to fill the

'Memorial of the former Princess Yung-t'ai of the Great T'ang.' Inscription from the Princess's tomb.

Engraved designs on the side of the Princess's memorial stone.

countryside; the jade flower is frozen in springtime . . .' The meaning of these phrases depends on their quotation of passages from ancient texts. A Chinese scholar has recently unravelled the passage to mean that Hsien-hui was still alive when her husband ('the coiled dragon') was dead, but that she was pregnant ('pearl' in the oyster) and died soon after in childbirth ('jade flower frozen'), while the child also died ('no fragrance'). Chinese memorial tablets, invaluable for archaeology of the post-Han period, very rarely falsify facts, but often obscure them. Even with this new interpretation, it is certain that Hsien-hui died in utter disgrace and was initially buried in obscurity, as were also her husband and brother.

The most obvious example of this sort of fate is the uncle, Li Hsien. He was the Empress Wu's own second son, born in 654 when she and the Emperor were on a visit to T'ai-tsung's mausoleum. But in 683 she banished him to Szechwan and ordered him to commit suicide the following year. He was buried in a place unrecorded. In the year 705, on Chung-tsung's return to the throne, restitution began and these three tombs have given important evidence of its process. Li Hsien's body was brought home to the royal cemetery in 706 and he was reburied as the Prince of Yung, a restored title. But originally he had been a Crown Prince and this title was not restored till 711. Then, one of his tomb's vertical shafts was re-opened, the body of a girl to whom he had been posthumously wedded was placed with his, the accoutrements of the tomb were revised to accord with his new rank and a new memorial stone for 'Crown Prince Chang-huai' was placed alongside that of the 'Prince of Yung'.

Li Ch'ung-jun and his sister were more immediately restored, also

117

Cross-section

The tomb of the Princess Yung-t'ai, buried 706.

1. Coffin chamber
2. Position of stone door
3. Ante-chamber
4. Position of wooden door
5. Memorial slab
6. Alcove
7. Shaft
8. Brick partitions
9. Wall painting
10. Entrance ramp
11. Position of iron axe
12. Coffin
13. Stone seat

Robbers' tunnel

Paved walk.

Remains of wall-painting on east side of entrance ramp with blue dragon of the east and guard at the gate.

Ground plan

0   5 M

in 706, perhaps because they were Chung-tsung's own children. Li Ch'ung-jun regained the title of Heir Apparent, Crown Prince I-te, and his sister was posthumously given the title Princess Yung-t'ai. Her memorial tablet suggests that her husband was buried with her and this is supported by the few bones which survive in the coffin.

These restitutions are partially recorded in the Official History of the T'ang, but not without some confusions. The excavations have at least shed light on one thorny problem which has long troubled the Chinese sense of ritual nicety. The History states that, on the Princess's reburial, 'her tomb was declared a royal tumulus (ling).' What does this mean? The memorial inscription merely calls it a 'tomb'. The three excavated tombs are all 'in attendance on Ch'ien-ling', the mausoleum of Chung-tsung's father. This is in the district called in the T'ang the 'Offering-to-Heaven District', which was reserved for royal burials. It lies some forty-five miles north-west of Sian. The burials' dominating feature is, of course, their great man-made mounds, but it is now becoming clear that the major distinction of an imperial tomb was the surrounding enclosure and its approach.

By the reign of Chung-tsung there was an elaborately ordained succession of sculptures to line the Spirit Road to the tomb and honour the rank of its occupant. The road began between two towers and stretched northwards for about six hundred yards between paired figures of men, lions, sheep and other guardian figures before it passed through the gates of an enclosure between two hundred and three hundred yards square. Slightly to the west of centre rose a stepped tumulus, and the road approached its sealed entrance between an intensified series of guardian figures. To the north, east and west of the enclosure other groups of sculpture were symmetrically ordered and the entire configuration was nearly a mile in length. The surroundings of the tombs of the Princess and her brother proclaim them royal tumuli and this status is carried through in the tombs' subterranean dimensions, which were regulated with equal rigour. Their uncle's tomb is somewhat smaller, and the records indeed state that he was not accorded a *ling*. The wording of the Princess's memorial suggests that her status was still under dispute and that the family did not dare to actually call her tomb a *ling*.

The year 706 must have been one of unique pomp and misery for the district of Offering-to-Heaven. The Empress Wu herself was buried with imperial honours in the same year that her victims were re-interred. The construction of these tombs, then as earlier, was an immense labour. When the Crown Prince Chang-huai's brother was buried, the labourers revolted and threw rocks at the supervisory officials until they all fled. There is a contemporary account of the burial of a certain Li I-fu, the 'human cat' who became one of the Empress Wu's wiliest advisers:

'... they commandeered labourers and ox-carts to carry the earth for the tomb mound, and the work did not cease even by night. Administrators of the six neighbouring districts were scared into sending more labour, and one official, terrified into intense work, died of exhaustion on the spot. When the coffin was interred, everyone competed in sending furnishings for the grave, the banners of their offerings came in an endless procession behind the spirit car ... the tents of sacrificial rites stretched along the road for forty miles ...'

The design of these graves was certainly derived from ancient practice and in ground plan they are quite similar to some Han dynasty tombs. But there are many features, such as the vertical shafts, about which we know very little. The number of these shafts is a feature plainly related to the status of the dead, as is also the length of the paved tunnel, the quantity and type of the funeral figurines and the decoration of the walls. The symmetrical niches at the bases of the shafts were filled with hundreds of the figurines, principally people and animals from the retinue of the dead. These could be delicate miniatures less than six inches in height, or impressive statues of over three feet. These larger figures, of warriors, monsters, horses and camels, often flanked the wood and the stone portals which successively protected the inner sanctum. Many of them are both great art and invaluable historical evidence, such as a horse in gold armour found in the tomb of the Crown Prince I-te. One aspect of the figurines which has attracted much interest is the frequency of foreign faces amongst them. T'ang China was a very cosmopolitan land and foreigners, then more than in any other age, were widely active in Chinese life. Their activities in fields such as the Palace Guard, entertainment and commerce are frequently reflected in the figurines. The strange features of these foreigners which most struck the Chinese, then as now, were their great noses and hairy faces; features which were a gift to the craftsmen in clay.

T'ang figurines are a rediscovery of the present century, revealed first through grave robbery but more recently through reputable archaeology. They were mostly, so far as we know, made especially for the grave and were quite unknown to later Chinese art collectors,

OPPOSITE
Court ladies in the palace garden. Engraved slab from the stone coffin of the Princess Yung-t'ai, 706 AD.

even in the gigantic collections of the Manchu emperors. Although they were but an overflow from the sculptural genius of the age, they have done much to remedy the great scarcity of surviving works that were carved for the living. Many were mass-produced from moulds, some were sculpted. Often they were undecorated, but sometimes casually splashed with yellow and green, occasionally with blue. Those decorated with gold from the Crown Prince's tomb are an exceptional discovery. The fresh vigour of these tomb wares, produced in great quantities and at necessary speed, is in remarkable contrast to the cool sophistication of the T'ang potters above ground, who had succeeded in producing a genuine, glass-like porcelain by the ninth century.

It was because the figurines were not the conventionally appreciated, and therefore valuable, ceramic ware that they were ignored by early robbers. In the three royal tombs, which had all been robbed, they were almost the only objects remaining. Robbers had entered the Princess's tomb down the last shaft and had, by accident or design, abandoned one of their number. His skeleton was found at the base of the shaft, an iron axe to hand and his last vain haul of gold, silver and jade scattered nearby, the only 'precious' objects still there. The other genuine treasures safe from removal were the wall-paintings and stone-engravings which covered almost every part of the tomb's interior. Unfortunately, the robbers' entries had let in mud and water, which had gravely damaged much of the painting. Even so, some sections survived remarkably well and their value is tremendous, for the T'ang was China's great age of wall-painting. Examples have survived in the cave temples at Tun-huang, but almost every other product of an art which once filled thousands of mansions and temples has long since perished.

The tomb walls were painted to reproduce a progress through the gates and into an imperial palace. Down the sloping sides of the entrance parade guards, with a halberd-stand holding exactly the number of weapons decreed by the resident's rank. Before the first shaft are painted gate towers; in the tomb of the Crown Prince I-te four magnificent structures clearly represent the series of four gates which led into the imperial palace. The entrance walls of the Crown Prince Chang-huai's tomb have an exceptionally interesting variety of scenes, such as visits by foreign ambassadors, polo, and hunting expeditions. Once inside the Inner Palace, the figures are restricted to privileged attendants. Among the most exquisite of these are the ladies in the palace gardens, engraved on the stone doors and coffin

Silver bracelet from the treasure of the Prince of Pin, early eighth century.

slabs of the Princess's tomb. The great majority of the inner figures are women, for during the first reigns of the T'ang dynasty the Inner Palace evolved a complicated establishment staffed almost exclusively by women. The occasional figures in male clothes which appear within the Princess's tomb are in fact young girls so dressed, a diversion well known in China for relieving the sexual tedium.

It was out of such a feminine context that the Empress Wu had burst forth in historical China's one brief flowering of female rule. It may be that the peculiar funerary privileges accorded the Princess Yung-t'ai were also due to the fact that her father, the Emperor Chung-tsung, was dominated by women; his own empress made a great, but fatal, effort to emulate the Empress Wu.

The Emperor Hsuan-tsung Ming-huang (Abstrusely Learned Ancestor and Enlightened Emperor) who came to the throne in 712, is particularly famous for his attachment to two concubines, Wu Hu-fei and Yang Kuei-fei. But he, nevertheless, became a ruler to equal T'ai-tsung in his greatness. Tradition has always held that Yang Kuei-fei was a perfection of succulent plumpness and that her form set a fashion. Certainly it is a curious fact that painted and modelled figures of the eighth century tend distinctly to the portly. Yang Kuei-fei's family, unfortunately, gained undue influence and her brother even became Prime Minister. This was just at the time when An Lu-shan, a rebellious general of Turkic origins, was raising a rebellion in the east and Hsuan-tsung's control suddenly collapsed. In 756 his court was driven into a brief exile and during the escape his resentful troops killed Yang Kuei-fei's brother and demanded the life of the beloved concubine herself. She was strangled, with the Emperor's dumb acquiescence. Soon afterwards he resigned the throne to his son and is said to have spent the rest of his days searching for her spirit. Less than fifty years later the eminent poet Po Chu-i wrote a song about the event, which so became one of China's favourite romances. The song ends: 'The span of heaven and the time of earth —they both shall have their end. But this remorse is everlasting.'

This passage of disaster through Ch'ang-an acquired an unexpected archaeological reality in the find that produced the dancing-horse saddle-bottle. This was in 1970, when two large earthenware jars unearthed in Sian disgorged a fantastic treasury of over a thousand pieces, including more than two hundred gold and silver vessels; foreign vessels of jade, onyx and other materials; coins from Persia, Byzantium and Japan; jewels and precious minerals for the preparation of medicines. The royal wealth of this hoard is explained by

Coiffure of court lady in the early eighth century. *See wall-painting facing page 112.*

123

the site of its discovery, which was the location of the mansion of the eighth-century princes of Pin.

When the Emperor fled the capital in 756, he took only Yang Kuei-fei, her family and a few other relatives, slipping out through the gates at the furtive dawning of a disastrous July day. When his officials came to present themselves for the morning audience, they found an empty throne. The rest of the royal clan woke up deserted, and most of them scattered in panic and disguise, as rebel troops broke into the city. There is little doubt that the amazing wealth buried in two innocent-looking jars is a relic of the frantic dismay that must have erupted in the Prince of Pin's mansion. No one returned to find the treasure. What happened to the Prince? Perhaps an answer is given in a poem by Tu Fu, a contemporary who himself suffered bitterly in the same rebellion, but who survived to become China's greatest poet. It is called *Grief for a Prince*, and says:

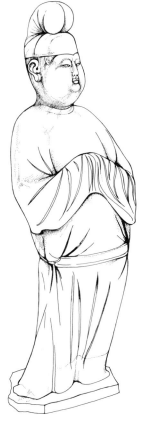

Court gentleman.
Tomb figurine of the
eighth century.

> 'To Ch'ang-an in the night came a white-headed raven, calling
>   from the city gate, heralding woe;
> Then flew over the houses to peck at the roofs of great mansions.
> The lords and ministers below awoke and fled to escape the
>   barbarians;
> Golden whips snapped, beating noble steeds till they died.
> The closest kin were parted in flight.
>
> 'I chanced on a piteous prince, weeping by the road—
> Precious gems and jewels under his coat.
> I asked him his name—he would not tell.
> Spoke only of harsh misery and begged me to take him as a slave.
> For days he has been a fugitive among thorns and brambles—
> Not an inch of his skin remains unscarred.
> The descendants of our first emperor have all a noble counten-
>   ance—
> A presence unmistakable for ordinary men.
>
> 'The kill-crazed wolf is in the palace—the dragon is in the wild.
> Oh prince! Guard well your treasured person.
> I dare not talk long beside this busy road—
> We can stand but a moment.
> Last night the east wind reeked of the blood it had drunk,
> Camels from the east fill Ch'ang-an . . .'

EPILOGUE: THE END OF CLASSIC CHINA

The reign of Hsuan-tsung (712–756) was the apogee of the T'ang dynasty. In the 750s the T'ang armies were finally beaten by the Arabs in both the far north-west and south-west, and when Hsuan-tsung's rule lay shattered under An Lu-shan's rebellion, the dynastic power had passed its peak. By the end of the eighth century other internal revolutions were now facing irrevocably forwards. The struggle for control of the government between an ancient elite raised by birth and a new elite raised by education turned finally in favour of the latter and the crucial (and in theory egalitarian) role of a bureaucracy with Confucian ideals was unalterably established.

In literature and the arts also the eighth century was a revolutionary period. Not only was it China's first 'renaissance', with people looking back beyond their immediate forbears to great eras like the Eastern Chin, but also the artistic giants of the day, men such as the poet Tu Fu, the calligrapher Yen Chen-ch'ing and the painter Wang Wei (who both reached ministerial rank in office), achieved a status which later generations never dared claim to surpass.

After the complete suppression, in 763, of An Lu-shan's rebellion, the government made many administrative changes, especially in the basis of tax revenue and the management of public works, which radically altered, mostly for the better, the relationship between government and the individual. For these and many other reasons the eighth century is a historical watershed, and the late T'ang has been called China's 'transition from the classic to the early modern period', which lasted until 1911. The China of this 'early modern period' developed the most sophisticated system of records and historical description known anywhere before the present century, and in this context we expect far less of archaeology than we have come to for the earlier periods.

Even so, students of T'ang and post-T'ang history are nowadays receiving information from archaeologists that is slowly improving these expectations. The recent work of Chinese archaeologists in excavations such as that of the Yuan dynasty capital indicates that the story of archaeology in the post-T'ang period will eventually be one of great importance.

Court lady. Tomb figurine of the eighth century.

125

BOOKS FOR FURTHER READING

ANDERSSON, J. G. *Children of the Yellow Earth: Studies in prehistoric China.* Cambridge, Mass.: The M.I.T. Press, nd.

Buddhist cave temples. Arts of China, Vol. II. Tokyo: Kodansha International Ltd., 1969

CHALFANT, F. H. *Three treatises on inscribed oracle bones.* New York: Paragon Book Reprint Corp., nd.

CHANG KWANG-CHIH. *The archaeology of ancient China,* Rev. and enl. ed. New Haven, Conn.: Yale University Press, 1971

CHENG TE-K'UN. *Prehistoric China.* Archaeology in China, Vol. I. Toronto: University of Toronto Press, 1961

————. *Shang China.* Archaeology in China, Vol. II. Toronto: University of Toronto Press, 1961

————. *Chou China.* Archaeology in China, Vol. III. Toronto: University of Toronto Press, nd.

CREEL, HERRLEE G. *Birth of China.* New York: Frederick Ungar Publishing Co., 1954

Cultural frontiers in ancient East Asia. Chicago, Ill.: Aldine Publishing Co., 1972

DAVIDSON, BLACK, et al. *Fossil man in China.* New York: AMS Press, Inc., nd.

HANSFORD, S. HOWARD. *A glossary of Chinese art and archaeology.* Elmsford, N.Y.: British Books Centre, Inc., 1973

Historical relics unearthed in New China. Hazelwood, Mo.: Great Wall Press, 1972

HSIA NAI, et al. *New archaeological finds in China.* Hazelwood, Mo.: Great Wall Press, 1972

LIANG, S. Y. *New stone age pottery from the historic site at Hsi-Yin-Tsun, Shansi China.* New York: Kraus Reprint Co., 1930

LOEHR, MAX. *Chinese bronze age weapons: The Werner Jannings Collection in the Chinese National Museum, Peking.* Ann Arbor, Mich.: The University of Michigan Press, 1956

LOEWE, MICHAEL. *Everyday life in Early Imperial China.* New York: G. P. Putnam's Sons, 1968; (paperback) New York: Harper & Row, Publishers

MOTE, F. W. *Intellectual foundations of China.* New York: Alfred A. Knopf, Inc., 1971

NEEDHAM, J. *Science and civilisation in China,* Vols. I–IV. Cambridge, England: Cambridge University Press, 1954–1971

Neolithic cultures to the T'ang dynasty. Arts of China, Vol. I. Tokyo: Kodansha International Ltd., 1969

SECKEL, D. *The art of Buddhism.* New York: Crown Publishers, Inc., nd.

STEIN, SIR AUREL. *On ancient Central-Asian tracks.* New York: AMS Press Inc., 1971

SULLIVAN, MICHAEL. *The cave temples of Maichishan.* Berkeley, Calif.: University of California Press, 1969

————. *A short history of Chinese art,* Rev. ed. Berkeley, Calif.: University of California Press, 1970

TREISTMAN, JUDITH M. *Prehistory of China: An archaeological exploration.* Garden City, N.Y.: Doubleday & Company, Inc., 1972

————. *Early civilization in China.* New York: McGraw-Hill Book Co., 1966

WRIGHT, A. F. *Buddhism in Chinese history.* Stanford, Calif.: Stanford University Press, 1970

INDEX